TEED OFF

TEED OFF

MY LIFE AS A PLAYER'S WIFE ON THE PGA TOUR

SHERRIE DALY

G

GALLERY BOOKS

new york   london   toronto   sydney

Gallery Books
A Division of Simon & Schuster, Inc.
1230 Avenue of the Americas
New York, NY 10020

First Gallery Books hardcover edition April 2011

GALLERY BOOKS and colophon are trademarks of Simon & Schuster, Inc.

Insert photos courtesy of the author.

For information about special discounts for bulk purchases, please contact Simon & Schuster Special Sales at 1-866-506-1949 or business@simonandschuster.com.

The Simon & Schuster Speakers Bureau can bring authors to your live event. For more information or to book an event, contact the Simon & Schuster Speakers Bureau at 1-866-248-3049 or visit our website at www.simonspeakers.com.

Designed by Davina Mock-Maniscalco

Manufactured in the United States of America

10   9   8   7   6   5   4   3   2   1

Library of Congress Cataloging-in-Publication Data

Daly, Sherrie.
Teed off : my life as a player's wife on the PGA tour / by Sherrie Daly.
p. cm.
1. Daly, John, 1966– 2. Golfers—United States—Biography. 3. Daly, Sherrie.
4. Wives—Biography. 5. PGA Tour (Association) I. Title.
GV964.D26A3 2011
796.352092—dc22
[B]
2010030863

ISBN 978-1-4516-1131-1

To my mom and dad,
the best parents in the world.

And to Austin and Little John,
my main men, who bring me
more happiness than they'll ever know.

And to A.T. and Michelle
for always having my back.

CONTENTS

CONTENTS

TEED OFF

PROLOGUE

I HATE GOLF. I'm serious. I've always thought golf was boring. I used to put it on the TV when I was a teenager because it made me fall asleep, and then I could sleep through being grounded. But when I married professional golfer John Daly in 2001 and started traveling with him on the PGA circuit, I decided I should try to make the best of it, even if it meant dressing all preppy and acting like a golf wife. I actually went out and bought a bunch of these boring collared shirts. That should tell you how committed I was to my marriage. I hate collared shirts, almost as much as I hate golf.

Little did I know that being a golf wife would mean fighting off strippers who think it's okay to be out on the golf course without any clothes on, like I found myself doing at a charity event in Arkansas about two years into my marriage. By then I'd gotten a clue that the world of professional golf isn't anything close to what it appears to be on TV. I'd learned that, actually, Dallas is the place that's known for strippers. The greens there aren't all nice and pretty, like you'd picture them to be. No, they look more like they're covered in garbage. They are. Strippers swarm the course alongside the real golf fans, acting like they're watching the game. Only they're wearing slutty high heels made out of rubber, and they're handing out to all of the players fliers for the strip clubs where they work. The grass is just littered with pieces of paper printed with pictures of those nasty strippers on them. Not only that, but I was a little disturbed when I first heard that a lot of the golfers do go to strip clubs. We even had a few who left their wives for strippers, plus a few wives who used to be strippers. They know who they are. I guess I shouldn't have worried so much about being preppy enough to fit in with the other wives.

The PGA has groupies, just like the ones who hang around the NBA. Golf sluts may dress in golf outfits, with those nerdy visors and argyle socks and sweater vests, and pretend they're interested in the game. But they're just whores in preppy clothes. They even go down the names on the money list, which makes their job easy by ranking all of the players according to their earnings for the year, and try to get with the richest guys they can. At least the NBA whores dress well.

Many of the guys aren't just players, they're *players*, and that means that when they're far away from their wives and kids, they get up to all kinds of bad behavior. Don't think for a second that Tiger's the only one who's ever strayed, or that the rest of them are devoted husbands. No way. Being rich and successful, these golfers have their choice of women, and being out on the PGA Tour means that they have plenty of opportunity to hook up with whomever they choose. When a golfer wants to sleep with a woman, all he has to do is write his number on the golf ball he's pretending to autograph for her.

So don't let the polo shirts and Dockers fool you. Professional golfers behave just as dirty as any other professional athlete or rock star. On top of all that, I had to go and fall for John Daly, the one they call Wild Thing because of his reputation for getting married (and divorced), losing hundreds of thousands of dollars at the casinos, drinking whiskey, trashing hotel rooms, and just generally getting into trouble—what we like to call "cutting up," where I come from in Memphis.

Now, this isn't all that surprising since, like a lot of women, I've always had a thing for bad boys. In my defense, though, John didn't act wild when we met, so I figured he'd already gotten all of that out of his system. Truth is, he was a little old, a little chubby, and a little blond—as in not my usual choice of tall, dark, and handsome. I thought I was a little out of his league at the time. I felt like *I* was the prize, not him. Some people have tried to run their mouths, saying I married him for his money. I don't think so. He had no money. He wasn't winning. He was kind of a has-been. And I've always had a good life. I drove a Mercedes before I met John, and I had plenty of generous friends and boyfriends. When I was twenty-one, I made a friend who had a private Learjet. So let's just say that when I started traveling around with John, that was not my first private plane, or my first rodeo with Vegas, or any of that other stuff.

John seemed like good marriage material. He was real sweet, and I figured I could run him. For a little while, right after we got married, I did have a good system going, where I made sure he focused on our family life and his golf. He was playing better than he had in years. He started winning, and he came back up the ranks again, making money and getting some big sponsorships.

There was just one problem, which John warned me about right from the get-go. He said, "If you ever see me drinking whiskey, leave."

Of course, by the time he picked up the whiskey again, after his mother died in 2002, we'd been married more than a year, and I wasn't about to just up and leave him. He still had that sweet side, and I loved him. Not only that, but where I come from, we take marriage serious. I'd been in love and had long-term boyfriends before, but I never married any of them—not even the father of my son Austin, who was eighteen months old when I met John— because I truly felt like marriage was a once-in-a-lifetime commitment. I didn't get married to get divorced. I really thought we'd be together forever. That's why it made me so mad that everyone else seemed to think it was some kind of a joke when John started cutting up real bad after his mother died. They even seemed to like him more the worse he behaved.

I put up with a lot from John during this time: trashed hotel rooms, wrecked homes and cars, nights he got so drunk he pissed the bed. Some nights he got so drunk he had to go to the hospital in an ambulance, and then his agents made up lies to pretend his drinking wasn't to blame. I usually just went along with it. But those strippers in Arkansas finally put me over the edge. Now, I have a problem with strippers to begin with. When my first son, Austin, was a baby, there was this one time his dad took a $10,000 check and got a limo with a bunch of his friends to go to the casino. Well, they wound up at this big strip club in Memphis called Platinum Plus, which ended up getting closed because so many dirty things went down in there. I had followed the limo in my own car because I was furious that he had spent so much money when we had a new baby to support. The door guys wouldn't let me in to confront Austin's daddy, so I was just sitting there in my car, fuming, with my sister trying to talk me down and Austin in his car seat. And then Austin took the biggest dump ever. I pulled right up to the club's front door, and I took that shit diaper and threw it, and it just splatted right on the entrance. That should pretty much tell you what I think about strippers. And it sure felt good.

So I wasn't happy when I heard that this charity event John was playing at included strippers as part of the day's festivities. And I certainly wasn't happy when John started drinking whiskey at seven o'clock that morning. But I tried to be fine with it, just to keep the peace. That was until I saw the strippers over at the tee box with John. Now, mind you, this was at a nice golf course, and they were raising money for the Make-A-Wish Foundation. There was not one but two girls, and they weren't wearing pasties or a bikini—or anything. They were buck naked, with these fat, cheesy butts. They weren't even cute. I could have made more money stripping, and I was then eight months pregnant with John's son, Little John. Not only was John standing by those girls. His hand was in his pocket, and he was getting money out. Giving it to strippers when he could have been giving it to Make-A-Wish kids. I was like: *You do not give* my *money to strippers.*

I was being driven to the bathroom by this redneck guy in a huge, four-wheel-drive golf cart. Only I forgot all about the bathroom when I saw the strippers.

"Go! Go!" I said, pointing in the direction of their ugly, naked asses.

"What's wrong?" the redneck said.

Like he needed to ask. I could tell he knew exactly why I was mad. So he started driving real slow, which made me even more heated. People were always protecting John and cleaning up his messes. The slower this guy went, the madder I got, thinking about how sick and tired I was of John's little fan club, and how they thought it was funny to encourage him to behave just as bad as he possibly could. They weren't the ones who had to deal with him when he staggered in drunk and out of control. No, that was his wife and kids.

It didn't help that I was watching the strippers prance and flirt around in front of John this whole time. And on top of that, all of this was being observed by a couple of hundred people, a lot of them friends and neighbors from our home in Dardanelle, Arkansas. I was going to have to see these people out around town and have them looking at me, thinking the whole time what a pig my husband was.

Well, that big stupid redneck couldn't stall forever, no matter how much he wanted to kiss John's ass. We finally got closer to John, and I realized that one of the strippers was a girl I'd seen earlier, with her shorts open, hanging around the tee box that John had been assigned to hit drives from that day. And when I say "shorts," they weren't anything more than a zipper.

"I just need an autograph," she kept saying.

"Get your autograph and get on down the road, girl," I said. "Scat."

Only when she finally did leave, she turned back toward me and smirked.

Now, you do not smirk at a big fat woman in a black spandex Donna Karan jumper that's about to pop, and whose baby, by the way, was so big that my guts had popped out and I had a hernia. I am not a happy fat person. I'm not happy pregnant. People can say they love it all they want. I don't. This was *not* the day to mess with me. And I swear, when I'm pregnant, I can box like a kangaroo.

So when I saw it was her again, I jumped out of the golf cart and started running up there to the tee box. Only I was wearing flip-flops, and I slipped, and then I tripped and fell. So not only was I mad, but I was embarrassed. That just made it worse. I went berserk. I grabbed that one girl, the one who had sassed me, and I choked her.

"I told you to keep your clothes on in front of my husband!" I said.

And then I grabbed the other girl's hair, and I swung her around every which way. And, of course, they weren't touching me because I was pregnant.

After that I was so worked up, I don't remember much of what happened. I don't think I punched John. But I've been told I punched nearly everyone else who was standing there giving those girls money. I punched our banker out, and he told my mom later that he had never been hit so hard in his life. I'm not sorry, either. Giving money to naked strippers that they could have been giving to sick kids.

And by the way, John was so drunk by then, he was already acting pathetic. He didn't need any help from me to make a spectacle. He was upset with me for going off on the naked girls. So he took a beer bottle, and right there in front of everyone, he threw it and hit me in my big pregnant stomach. And then he just left me standing there, totally shocked and embarrassed. Somebody else had to drive me up to our bus in a golf cart. The whole time, no one asked if I was okay. It was like he could act as nasty as he wanted to, and nobody said anything about it because he was John Daly.

People wonder how I could have put up with all of that, and the even worse stuff that he did to me over the next few years, leading up to the night in 2007 when he acted so bad to me that he lied and said I stabbed him, just to cover it all up. Well, there were plenty of times when we were happy, for one thing. We could have had a real nice life. The perks of being John Daly's wife, or of being the wife of any player on the PGA circuit, were about as good as they get. And when things were bad, like a lot of women whose husbands get up to no good, I had a real knack for pretending that things were different than they were. And of course, John was always real sorry afterward, and he could explain away just about anything. And when you're in it, and raising little ones, you're just trying to get from day to day and avoid a divorce for the sake of the kids. So I was always like, okay, I'm going to give this one more shot. Maybe I was stupid to be so forgiving, but I still think that was the right thing to do.

Because I do think it's possible for people to be sorry and to change. Maybe that's because, with me, when I do something, I admit it. Because I'm not going to lie: I'm not perfectly innocent myself. And if I'm going to write this book, I have to tell on myself too. So here it is. The other reason I stayed with John for as long as I did is that I thought it was my karma. When I was younger, I ran around, and I didn't think too much about the guys I ran around with. If a married guy said his wife was a bitch, I figured she probably was, and we'd go off and party, and that was fine with me. I screwed around with other women's husbands. I'm not proud of it, but I did.

I never really thought too much about it, until this one lady called my house. She didn't yell, but it was almost worse, how hard and cold her voice was.

"I just want to know," she said. "Were you with my husband?"

I actually hadn't slept with her husband, but I did hang out with him, so she had every reason to believe I had been up to no good. And like I said, it could have just as well been a call from some other wife whose husband I had been with.

I've never forgotten what she said to me then. I used to think about it a lot during the times when John would drive off for days at a time, and I didn't know where he was, and he wouldn't call me or even answer his phone.

"Just remember one thing, little girl," she said. "You'll be married, and you'll be sitting home with your kids one day. You just remember me, because you'll get yours."

So there was a long time when I felt like I was getting mine, and that I even deserved the things John did to me because it was my payback. But after I got it like ten times a million harder, I finally thought to myself, *Okay, anybody I've ever done any-*

thing to, all of you know I got paid back with John Daly. With a bonus.

Whether it was karma or just something crazy that happened when John and I got together, we had quite a time—good and bad—during the nearly ten years we were married. The truth is, I still root for him. And don't think it's because I'm getting any money from him, either, because I'm not. I loved John. He was my husband, and he'll always be the father of our son, Little John. For a while there, he was a good father to my first son, Austin, too. I also got to travel the world, meet presidents and movie stars, and do some serious damage at Gucci with my credit card. I'll always be grateful for that, even though it hasn't been as glamorous in recent years. Not with my sex addict husband publicly rubbing my face in his new relationship with some old Hooters employee, while I've been stuck at home, learning how to steal utilities and make a meal out of Taco Bell.

Even when he left me without any child support, took away my car, and had my house foreclosed on, I never had any desire to trash John. I didn't care if I saw money, as long as my sons were taken care of. But I couldn't abide people thinking I was this crazy woman who went around stabbing people, like John said I did. So I gave him a choice during the divorce. I said if he'd just go to the media and admit he'd lied about what really happened that night, I'd walk away with nothing and I'd never tell my side of the story. Well, he just couldn't do it. So, as John used to say, grip it and rip it. The story is coming out. And the first thing I've got to say, after everything I've learned, is that I stand corrected: The world of professional golf may be many things, but it's anything but boring.

one

THE RIGHT SHOES AND THE RIGHT ATTITUDE REQUIRED

I T ALL STARTED, like so many important moments in a woman's life, with a really good blowout. If I hadn't given myself one that morning, I might never have met John, and this whole story might never have happened. We hadn't crossed paths before, even though we both lived in Memphis and knew a lot of the same people. A bunch of my friends had houses in TPC Southwind, which is the gated golf community where John lived at one point before we got married, and where I live now. I was even invited to parties at his house before, through our mutual acquaintances, but I'd always said no thanks. I was working for my dad at the time, selling cars at his car lot. My friend Kent, who owned another dealership in Marion, Arkansas, was good friends with John and had tried to introduce us a bunch of times. I'd always passed. I mean, I really could have cared less about meeting John Daly. It wasn't just because I wasn't into golf, either. "I don't want to meet any more rednecks," I said. "I'm not interested."

But when Kent invited me to go along with him to the St. Jude Classic in June 2001, I finally caved. Not because I had changed my mind about meeting John. But if I straighten my hair and get myself all done up, then I've pretty much got to go out to lunch, or at least go somewhere I'll be seen. I'll keep making everyone I know crazy until I finally find someone to go with me. On this day, no one would even answer their telephones, so I was getting real bored and restless. I wanted to go out, even though it wasn't like I was looking so hot or anything. In fact, I was especially overweight for me, like 138 pounds. (Just to put this into perspective, I didn't weigh but 136 pounds right before my son was born.) So I was real chunky for me, with these big, chubby cheeks. And I was wearing my fat pants, which were these black pants that were the only thing that looked halfway decent, an orange tank top, and some red flip-flops. But my hair was done, and I was ready to go out. So when Kent finally picked up his phone and told me he was going to Southwind to check out this annual charity event, I figured it was better than sitting around all day doing nothing.

I met Kent over at Southwind, which is on the east side of Memphis in an upscale suburb called Germantown. We walked down to the course, and it was a real nice day. The event is a big deal in Memphis, so the whole place was packed, and we spotted a bunch of people we knew. We stood and watched the play for a while, and then John made the turn, which is right there at the tenth hole. He came over to say hello, and Kent introduced us. Right away I was struck by the fact that John wasn't anything like I had thought he would be. I was expecting this big scruffy redneck voice, and he was very soft-spoken, with this sort of gentle nature to go along with his way of speaking. And he had big blue eyes that were real pretty. I still wasn't exactly interested in him, or anything like that, but he was a lot cuter, and much sweeter, in person than I had imagined. We followed him for a few holes. I knew John was supposed to be some kind of real good player, but I couldn't tell from what I saw, and I wasn't any more riveted by golf than I'd ever been. But I was glad to be out of work for the afternoon and having a nice time.

Afterward, we all met up in the parking lot, and a little group of us ended up just kind of hanging out there for a while, kidding around and talking. John wasn't flirting with me, exactly, but I noticed that he was paying me a little extra attention. It was all right by me, but I didn't think too much about it.

I ended up leaving Kent and John and going off with some friends who worked at the Silver Star Hotel and Casino, where I used to hang out quite a bit. John was staying at the Horseshoe Tunica, and he'd decided to have a little party in his room that night. He eventually called one of these mutual friends and said that he wanted me to come over. By that point I was with my good friend Lauren, and we were already on our way down to the casino, so we said we'd stop by John's room. But then we decided to go to the Peabody instead, which is this historic hotel in downtown Memphis that's known for having ducks that swim around in a fountain by the bar. But once we were on our way to the Peabody, we felt bad ditching John after we said we'd meet up with him, so we changed our plans again. We must have turned the car around at least two times, and we were just giggling, laughing, and having fun the whole way there.

By the time we got to the Horseshoe, there were maybe a dozen people partying with John in his room. He'd been gambling and had won quite a bit of money. Plus he'd played very well at the tournament that day. And as I soon learned, just how well John does on the course, and at the slots, is often the key to whether he's a whole lot of fun or the source of a whole lot of broken glass.

Even back then, I knew he had a reputation for being wild. I didn't read the newspaper much, so I wasn't aware of the details, but my friends who were his neighbors had told me things, and I knew there was always something or other going on with him. But that didn't scare me at all. Like a lot of other women, I've always thought I could tame the wild ones, and the challenge of trying to do so was part of the fun for me. Plus, John was real nice, and it seemed like maybe all of that craziness was behind him. He was real attentive to me all night, making sure I had a drink and was having a good time. And then, as it got late, everyone started leaving, until it was finally just the two of us. We sat on the couch together and had a drink, and he decided he wanted to come clean to me about everything. He told me he'd been married three times, and that he had two daughters he didn't see as much as he would have liked. He really seemed to be sorry for the mistakes he'd made in the past, and to be trying to live better now. I looked into those big blue eyes of his, and I believed every word of it.

I thought I'd finally found someone who was going to be good to me and give me a high quality of life. I ended up spending the night, and we had a real nice time. More than that, I'm not going to say, thank you very much. I'm not someone who believes in talking about what goes on in the bedroom. That might sound funny, given that I was about to marry a sex addict and get involved in everything that's imaginably wild and crazy. But back then, before the strippers and Hooters girls, I still thought he was a nice guy. So let's just leave it at that.

I left the next day and went to Pickwick Lake, which is about thirty minutes from the Horseshoe. I was with a bunch of my other friends, drinking and carrying on.

"Where have you been?" they were asking me. More like teasing me, because they could tell from the way I was acting that something was up.

"I've been out with this guy, John Daly," I said.

None of the girls knew who John was. But the guys sure knew a thing or two.

"John Daly, the golfer?" they said.

"I know he's got a real bad reputation," I said.

They started giving me a hard time about him and how nuts he was.

"I think I'm going to marry him," I said.

I was laughing when I said it, like just kidding around. But somehow, I knew that I really meant it.

The weird thing, which I didn't know at the time, was that John had said the same thing to Kent right after he met me at the golf course.

"I'm going to marry her," John had said, just like that.

Later on, after we did get married, John and I put it all together, and we laughed with our friends about it. Somehow, he and I both knew it was right.

What I didn't know was that John may have seemed like he was coming clean about his past, but he had a way of telling only as much as was convenient for him and leaving out, or covering up, anything he didn't feel like talking about. When he'd told me about his three ex-wives, he also mentioned that he was currently engaged to a woman named Shanae who lived in Dallas. But he gave me a line about her cheating on him, and he had already been planning to break it off with her. He made her out to be so bad that I didn't think much about the fact that he was technically cheating on her with me; it sounded like it was already over between them.

He failed to tell me, as I was leaving Memphis to spend the day at Pickwick Lake, that Shanae was flying in from Dallas to see him. And though he may have already made up his mind that he was going to marry me, as far as Shanae knew, he was still very much planning to marry her. The St. Jude Classic was still under way, so she was walking around the course with John, totally clueless the whole time that he'd been with me the night before and that he'd decided I was going to be his fourth wife, even though she was still wearing the five-karat diamond ring he had given her the previous year. There was even an article in the local newspaper about John Daly's fiancée and her big diamond ring.

I didn't know a thing about it. Not that I would have cared, to be honest with you. I'm sorry if the way everything went down was painful for Shanae, but it was like that was just the way it had to be. I don't know quite how to explain it, but it was like things with John just had this momentum to them, and I never had any doubt in my mind that we were going to get married, no matter what obstacles might seem to stand in the way. Plus, he could be very convincing, and so it never occurred to me that there was any side to the story other than the one he'd told me, about Shanae being a cheater and no good. Anyhow, after the tournament, he went out of town, as I later learned, to break things off with her. The next thing I knew, he was back in Memphis, staying at the Grand Casino, and I was seeing him every day.

Now, I had a few things to take care of myself before I was free to become Mrs. Daly. For starters, I had two really nice boyfriends at the time. My son Austin was nineteen months old, and I'd never married his dad, so I was a single mom. And both of these guys really loved my kid, which was a big part of why I liked them. And both of them were very upset when I broke things off. In fact, one of them called me after I'd met John but before I had a chance to let him down easy.

"I'm going to John Daly's Make-A-Wish event," he said. "Do you want to go with me?"

"I'm sorry," I said. "I'm already going."

"With who?" he said.

"John Daly," I said.

I could tell he was upset from the way his voice sounded all tight and weird.

"Oh my God, he's going to love you," he said. "You're going to end up marrying him. I'll never see you again."

"No, don't be silly," I said.

But my ex-boyfriend ended up being right about at least one of the things he predicted.

John was always real active with the Boys and Girls Clubs of America and the Make-A-Wish Foundation, as I later learned, because of a young leukemia patient he'd met and been inspired by at a 1994 Make-A-Wish event. And his annual Boys and Girls Clubs fundraiser, which he hosted at the golf course he had first played on near his boyhood home in Dardanelle, Arkansas, was always a big deal for him. Once we were married, it was a total nightmare for me, as something about being back home brought out the worst in John, and I've never seen him behave so bad as he did at those events. But that first year, he was on his best behavior. I went up there to Arkansas with him, and we all stayed at his house, which is on the golf course, and we had a lot of fun. I had Austin with me. And John had both of his daughters—Shynah, from his marriage to ex-wifey number two, and Sierra, from his marriage to ex-wifey number three—who were staying with him for the summer. And his mom and dad, and his brother and sister-in-law, who is one of my best friends to this day, all lived in houses nearby, so I met them, and we all got along real well. I was happy, and I thought I would be for a long time.

After that, I started traveling with John, and because Austin was so young at the time, he went everywhere with us. John was real good with Austin, and it was like we were this instant family. John was very nice and attentive to me and to my son, and I couldn't have asked for anybody better.

A few weeks after we met, I went to my first PGA event, which was at the Colorado Golf Club outside of Denver. I still remember that they make the best chocolate milkshakes there. I'm a big eater, and my mom has even said that sometimes she swears the only time she sees me smile is when I've just eaten something delicious, so a lot of times I remember a place by the meal we had there. Sometimes it's all I can remember of a place, because of how much we traveled and how all of the cities and golf courses started to blend together.

Now, when we got to Denver, I had never walked a golf course before. Even in my fat pants, I was relatively in shape, but when you've never walked a golf course before, let's just say it's a long way to walk. On top of that, the altitude was killing me. So I was going along on the first day, trying to pay attention to how John was playing, all eager to show him how supportive and sweet his new girlfriend could be. But I was about to pass out. I remember going up this hill, and I literally came close to falling to my knees. I've never had that feeling before. It was horrible.

There was a man in front of me who had a bottle of water in his hand.

"Excuse me," I said. "Can I please have a drink of your water?"

I actually drank from a complete stranger, and I finished his whole bottle of water too, every last drop. I felt like I was dying.

And that's not all. I swore up front that if I was going to tell on John in this book, it was only fair to tell on myself too. So I've got something to come clean about. The other reason I had such a hard time during the first day of the tournament had nothing to do with the altitude. It had to do with how much I hated golf and golf clothes, and the stupid fashion choice this inspired me to make.

Now, I was totally nervous about fitting in with the other golfers' wives and girlfriends when I first started traveling with John. I wanted to be dressed right and look cute, but I didn't know anything about golf, so I had no idea what that meant. And I didn't know anyone in that world, so I had no one to ask.

So, yes, I had bought some collared shirts to look the way I thought a golf wife should look. And, yes, I was wearing my fat pants because I was still real chunky back then, and they were all I could fit into. But I was determined that my shoes were going to be cute. So I had on these open-toed, high-heeled Donald Pliner sandals that I really liked. Well, you try walking in wet grass in open-toed, high-heeled sandals. My feet were sliding through my shoes, and my toes were all cut up and covered in blisters. I swear, they should have Band-Aid stands out there on the fairway. I have no idea how I even lasted so long, but by the ninth hole I was in the clubhouse, buying myself socks and spiked golf shoes. Now, collared shirts are bad enough, but I truly never thought I'd be caught dead in golf shoes, and let me tell you, I never will be again. I sure learned my first valuable lesson about golf that day: Footwear is crucial. I said good-bye to my heels and even my cute flip-flops. Instead, I soon bought tennis shoes in every color and matched them to my outfits from then on out.

Between my impractical shoes and the elevation, I was far from the polished golf wife I'd hoped to be. I was a complete and total mess. By the time John got done playing, he couldn't help but laugh at me. Not in a mean way, but because I looked so miserable, and I was so wide-eyed about something that had been his life for fifteen years.

"I told you to be careful with the altitude and all that stuff," he said.

Luckily, I soon got help from some of the other players' wives. Golfers travel more than other professional athletes—there were years in our marriage when John was home less than thirty days out of 365—and so their wives are more likely to go along with them than in the NBA or whatever they have in baseball. During my first months traveling with John, he and Austin and I were really excited to be this new little family unit that did everything together, so I didn't spend too much time with the wives. But the ones that I did meet sure saved me. There was so much to learn, and they were so good to me. I truly would have been lost without them. Like, for example, I remember I had Austin with me one day when I first married John, and I was trying to push his baby carriage across the course, which isn't any easier than walking through grass in Donald Pliner heels. Plus, I was finding that I was not in as good shape as I'd thought I was, but I was not going to miss a hole of golf, because I was the new girlfriend. Mia Parnevik, who's married to Jesper Parnevik, came up to me.

"Why do you push the baby every week?" she said. "You should take him to the daycare."

I didn't know that there was a daycare, and John never would have thought to tell me. In fact, the PGA does right by its players and their families, and they have a really nice daycare and school set up at every tournament. And it's not strangers in each city, either. A group of girls travel with the PGA, so they'll be familiar to the kids, and they bring the same toys. Austin went to the daycare for five years, and there were a few girls who worked there the whole time, so they basically helped to raise him. The PGA really puts a lot of thought and money into making the players' families feel comfortable and welcome out on the road. And every time a baby is born, they always send gifts and flowers. It's really a shame that John, or Tiger, or whoever, couldn't be happy family guys because the Tour caters so much to that. There's no denying that all of the travel is hard, and there's a lot of pressure, but with the money that can be made, and the luxury, it could be a really beautiful life.

There was a lot to learn about how to take advantage of all of the perks and how to travel as much as we did with small kids. Marci Blake, who's married to Jay Don Blake, was like my own personal PGA Tour guide, and we became really good friends and are still close to this day. Some of the other wives I met right away were Diane, who's Frank Lickliter's fiancée—I don't think they've ever married. She was extremely kind. I always thought of Diane as the perfect Tour wife, so I kind of used her as the model of what to wear: tasteful, because I like to dress up and look nice, but not too preppy, maybe tailored slacks with a collared shirt (I know, I know), which I had gotten John's logo sewn onto.

We traveled constantly, right from the beginning. We went to the British Open and all around the States. In between John's matches and appearances, we went back to his house in Arkansas. One day during the last week of July, we were there with Austin, and John had his girls there too. It was one of those days when there were a lot of kids running around the house, and there was just a lot going on. John and I were both passing through the back bedroom at the same time when all of a sudden, he turned to me and stopped me from walking out into the next room.

"I've got to be in Vegas for an outing on Friday," he said. "Do you want to go with me and get married?"

"Well, I guess so," I said.

I know that doesn't sound very romantic. But it all happened so naturally; I think it hadn't really sunk in what a big deal this was.

"Okay," he said. "What kind of ring do you want?"

"It doesn't matter," I said. "Whatever."

And that was it. Fifty-three days after I met John, we were married.

I guess it wasn't much of a proposal. I don't think we even kissed. It wasn't that we didn't love each other. It was just that we had become this wonderful family without even having to try, and it almost felt like we were already married. We went to the jewelry store when we were back in Memphis, and John gave me a real nice four-karat square-cut diamond. I thought it was beautiful, but John had other ideas.

"It's not big enough," he kept saying. "I want you to have a five-karat."

A few months later, he told me that he needed to get my ring cleaned—that old trick—and when he brought my ring back, it had a new and even bigger diamond on it that was something like 5.8 karats. John was always buying me jewelry and always doing me kindly like that. At least in the beginning.

The whole wedding process was as laid back as the proposal, but I felt happy and clear that I was making the right decision. He went and got a ring for himself, and I went and got a dress. I went to this store called Ballew in Memphis and bought something right off the rack. We met back up and went to the airport. I have a funny picture of John carrying my dress and a case of beer. That was pretty much it. He was doing an outing for Bally's Casino, so we flew to Vegas on their private plane. My friend Lauren was there and John's friend Steve Mata, who worked at this golf company called Titleist. We had all been at the British Open together, so the four of us were real comfortable around each other. There was a lot of drinking. There was a lot of money. There was a lot of everything. Lauren and I would get up in the morning and start drinking mimosas and shopping at the casino. While we were doing that, John was gambling. And, for once, everything he touched was magic. Whether he was playing blackjack or the $100 slots, everything would be $100,000 or $300,000. It was just crazy. Lauren and I went and met him the night before I got married, and all of us were drinking champagne and eating dinner down by the slot machines. They don't let most people do that, but the casino set up a special table for John. What they probably wanted to do was close him down because the machines would not stop winning for him. But they treated him like royalty, and he kept playing. By the time he was done and we went up to our room, we had more than a million dollars spread out on the bed, just like in a movie or something. It was wild. I don't even think it really registered with me. It didn't seem real.

John loved to gamble. And he loved to win. So that put him in a real good mood and that whole trip was magical, even though the actual wedding was simple. We had our ceremony at the chapel at Bally's Las Vegas, which looked like a pretty little church. I carried flowers and John looked handsome in a cream-colored blazer and slacks, which was dressed up by his standards. We said traditional vows in front of my mom and a handful of friends, including a few casino hosts and a bookie, and we were newlyweds.

For a long time, John thought of me as a good luck charm. Now, a lot of other people, including his ex-wifey number three, had different ideas about me. They liked to say I was just marrying him for his money.

But the thing was, I didn't need his money. And he had far less at his disposal than it might have seemed, even when he was winning.

He had broken it down for me when we first met.

"I've been married three times," he said. "I gave this one

everything. I gave that one everything. I have to pay $20,000 a month in child support. I have a little money, but not much."

"Well, is there *anything* left for me?" I said. "I don't require a lot. But is there just a little bit left?"

"Oh yeah," he said. "There's a little for you."

There may have been enough money for him to take on a fourth wife and stepchild. But there was also a lot of gambling debt. So in order to avoid taking that on as my own, and to shut up everyone who was calling him and telling him not to get married again and accusing me of being a gold digger, I asked for a prenup. We verbally agreed that it would go away when we had a child, or after a couple of years. I figured it was the best thing for me. That way, when I walked into a room, or I met his agents or sponsors, I could feel normal, instead of as if everyone was talking about me. Of course, we were all drinking when we did the prenup and neither of us actually read it. I never even looked at it until three years later, when I was filing for a divorce the first time. Let's just say now, that's not a good idea.

But we were happy, and in love, and I didn't think too much about it. I had also learned, even before we were married, that there were certain conversations about money that were off limits. One night I was with John at the Grand in Memphis, and he was playing slots with these $500 chips. So he'd put in $500, and then maybe another $500, and that would be one pull. I almost couldn't stand there and watch him do it. All I could think about was how much I could buy for the house, and for Austin, or even just how many pairs of shoes I could get for myself with that kind of money. I mean, I might spend a lot of money, but I come home with bags to show for it, and I'm usually buying something that's a timeless piece that I'm going to have forever. Throwing it away like that seemed like such an insane waste.

I'm not afraid of a lot in this life, though, so I decided to speak up.

"You know, every time you drop one of those, that's my rent and utilities for the month," I said. "That's so much money. Do you ever want me to say something?"

"If you're ever doing without something, then tell me to stop gambling," he said. "But if not, then don't interrupt me while I'm playing."

Well, as long as I went along with what John wanted, he was very good to me, and I never was doing without something. Or, more truthfully, there was never a time I was doing without something when my parents weren't kind enough to step in and lend us some money. So I never said anything about his gambling again. And even that first conversation wasn't an argument or anything like that. It was more like I was asking him some questions and getting some facts straight about what kind of boundaries we needed to have. In the beginning we were winning, so I didn't think I'd ever really have to say anything about his gambling. In fact, our winning streak didn't show any sign of slowing down, even after we got home from Vegas.

Our friend John Sisinni, who was the casino host at the Horseshoe, planned us a big reception for all of the friends and family who weren't able to be at our actual wedding. It was a lot of fun, except I was actually late to my own party because John and I were playing slots, and we won around $300,000, and the machine wouldn't stop paying out. That's how big we won. Again. I didn't even have the chance to change before I went into the reception hall, and there are now keepsake pictures of me wearing a tank top and these ridiculous pants with big red roses on them. I didn't look good at all. But it was a great party. It was at the Horseshoe's nightclub, Bluesville, and the casino's owner, Jack Binion, paid for everything, which was so generous. My parents didn't have to spend a dime. There were about a thousand guests, a big buffet and an open bar, and Hootie & the Blowfish played. They were good friends with John, and at one point before we got married, he had been out of town somewhere with them and had them on the telephone to me singing that "I Go Blind" song. See, John could be romantic. And I had graduated from high school in the 1990s, so they were a big deal band for me. It was like a fairy tale to have them playing at my wedding party. Of course, looking back, they also played at Tiger and Elin's special day, and Elin and I could easily trade notes and sex therapists' numbers now. So, even though I love each and every one of them as people, maybe Hootie & the Blowfish are bad luck as a wedding band.

There didn't seem to be anything but the best possible luck on the horizon for the first year of our marriage. In late August, we went to Germany for the BMW International Open. This was a major event for John. On the PGA circuit, the important tournaments are called Majors, and John hadn't won one of these since 1995. Since this was in Europe, it wasn't quite as big of a deal, but almost. And after several years of losing, which had seen his ranking drop to that of the 507th player in the world—which, I mean, come on, there can't be many more people than that even playing golf professionally, can there?—he was on his way back up to the top. Everything went great from the first day that we arrived. John was playing well, so he was in a good mood, which made me happy. And the people who ran the tournament were so welcoming to us.

The only problem was that, sure, I had learned some things during that first disastrous event in Denver, but I still hadn't walked that many golf courses, and so I was just lost from the get-go. Plus, here we were in a foreign country, where everyone was speaking a different language from me. I would be watching John, and then I'd go off with one crowd when they started moving, and by the time I'd realized they were going the wrong way, it was too late for me to cut across the green like I was supposed to do. I'd see John playing all the way over there, across the grass, and I'd be standing on this other hole, so far away, and wondering how I was going to get back across to him. And that was on the good days.

Now, the last day of the tournament wasn't such a good day. It had *started out* great. John was leading the tournament, and he was about to win an important event for the first time in six years. With his new wife cheering him on. It was a big story. And it was a big moment in our relationship. I was his Lady Luck back then, and after he played so well the first day, he figured it must be the outfit I was wearing, which was a pink shirt with his logo on it, and my trusty fat girl black pants. So, the next day, I put on the same thing. Actually, I wore that exact outfit for three days in a row.

After I got dressed at the hotel that morning, I went through my bag, which John had packed for me. He's a neat freak to begin with, plus he traveled so much that he could literally pack for two months in one suitcase. I got together everything I'd need for the day, so I'd be ready to leave for the course.

We went downstairs and got in our courtesy car, and while we were driving to the BMW, things started getting weird. I turned to John.

"How many cars do you see in front of us?" I asked.

"What?" he said.

There were three beige cars all lined up in front of us.

"Why are there three cars in front of us?" I asked.

"What is wrong with you?" he said.

"I don't know," I said. "I'm just seeing things."

I turned and looked at him more closely.

"Oh, God, I see two of you," I said.

Then I got what had happened.

"I think I took the wrong pill," I said.

I usually kept my Phentermine, which I was taking to lose my extra weight, so I could wear something other than black pants again someday, in my purse. And my Ambien, which I needed because I couldn't sleep at all overseas, went in my overnight bag. But because John had packed my stuff for me, everything was all switched around.

I was dozing off in the car, but there was no time to go back. And when we got to the course, John didn't want to leave me alone, but he had to go and tee off.

"Just help me get to the clubhouse," I said.

He half carried me in there, and I was basically sleeping on the table.

I started calling people from home, hoping they could tell me what to do.

The best thing we could come up with was that I should take a diet pill and drink an espresso, which I recall tasted terrible, in hopes of waking myself up. I couldn't be asleep when he won the tournament.

So I did all of that, and it helped some. But I was still real out of it.

John told me later that I walked outside and headed right over to where he was hitting the ball with his three wood. I guess I thought I was being supportive. Only I was basically sleepwalking, and when he swung back, he just about hit me in the head. I got myself to where I was at least able to walk and follow him around while he played. But then, all of a sudden, he was on the eighteenth hole, and I was all the way across the lake. So I was standing there like an idiot, wondering how I was going to get over to where he was. Well, I didn't. So when he won the biggest tournament of our marriage, and one of the biggest of his career, I wasn't even there to run up and hug him. I had to walk up a few minutes late because of the Ambien. At least we were getting along real well in those days, so we just laughed about that one. See, this is good for me to remember: There *were* happy days together.

two

JOHN, JOHNNY, AND JD

O NE OF THE FIRST THINGS I learned about being a PGA wife is that it comes with some rewards. When a husband does well at a major tournament that has a big purse, the wife usually receives an equally major piece of jewelry. After John won the BMW Classic he bought me a twenty-karat tennis bracelet covered in beautiful emerald-cut diamonds. And that wasn't all. In the first few months of our marriage, he gave me something like sixty karats of diamonds.

Between the money he earned once he started playing well again, and the winning gambling streak we had when we got married, he was able to pay down a bunch of his gambling debts. We even had enough money left over that John was able to do something for himself. He hates flying and was always a nervous wreck when we had to travel, just covered in a cold sweat. So he wanted to buy himself a tour bus that he could drive around to tournaments and outings. It was a lot of money, around $800,000, but he really wanted one, so I said he should get it. He'd earned it. Our first bus was used, but it was actually a very good bus, equipped with a bedroom, shower, and everything we needed for a life on the road. John was in heaven. But for me, even in later years, when we were on our biggest, fanciest bus, which cost nearly two million dollars, I was never so sure about the lifestyle.

Things were relatively nice and calm back then, but I still needed to take Valium to avoid having a nervous breakdown while John was driving. Even when he wasn't driving drunk, which he did all the time in later years, he was a crazy man behind the wheel. I can't tell you how many times I'd find him with the speedometer needle bottomed out, which meant he was going well over a hundred miles an hour. And it was crowded on the bus, especially when we were hauling around his caddie and his best friend, who he hired to drive for him and kiss his ass. Plus, during the summer, we often had his two daughters with us too. I wanted to get to the tournament and check into a hotel room, but John wanted to park the bus at a campground and stay there the whole time, like a hillbilly jamboree.

The good thing about having a bus on the PGA circuit was that some of the other players I really liked, including Davis Love, Jay Don and Marci Blake, and Heather and Marco Dawson, had buses too. Heather actually drove their bus, which I never dared to do.

But I loved seeing her behind the wheel. She and Marci were my really good friends. We'd park near each other at the campground, and cook out and relax between events.

Life settled into a routine. Nearly every week we would drive from tournament to tournament, and it was just like hauling our home with us, so we cooked and ate most of our meals on the bus. John needed to get into town on Monday or Tuesday so he could practice. While he was at the course, I usually did something with Austin, like go to a toy store or a museum, and when John was done playing golf for the day, we might go have lunch somewhere together. Just normal family stuff. Wednesday was what they call a pro-am, which is a PGA-organized fundraiser. Sponsors would usually play on those days. Or let's say someone's dad and his three buddies wanted to play with the members of the PGA Tour, they could pay $10,000 apiece to do so, knowing that their money was going to a good cause.

And then, on Thursday, the tournament would begin. They would play on Thursday and Friday, and then, at the end of the day Friday, they'd make what was called the cut. This varied from tournament to tournament, but it usually consisted of the top seventy players, plus any ties. Players who missed the cut were out and didn't get any money. But those who made the cut moved on to the next round and played on Saturday and Sunday. Whoever played the best won, obviously, and would take the tournament's purse. To decide on the rest of the payouts, they worked their way down the list of finishers, with each person making slightly less money. That's why it was so important when John started making the cuts again. And when he knocked off the crazy behavior he'd been known for in the past. There are, in fact, official rules about behavior, and players can get disqualified and fined for acting up on the course. When we were first together, John stopped throwing his clubs around and breaking them. I had told him it was embarrassing and it didn't look good. And when he was playing well, he didn't get caught up in all that nonsense.

The press really did call me Lady Luck back then in some of the articles written about John. As soon as I came around, he was always making cuts. They're real big into statistics in golf, and according to his numbers from 2001 to 2006, which were the years we were happiest, he made more money than at any other time in his career. Ever since we got married, he has played in the Masters, which he certainly hadn't done in the years right before 2001. And pretty soon his ranking was up to around thirty-seven, so I do take some credit for that. We had a good little program going.

Winning tournaments was important. But the real money was in sponsorships. When we first met, John didn't have any substantial ones left because of how bad he'd been playing. But as he started coming back up, companies became interested in him again, and he got some big contracts. Being sponsored meant wearing the company's logo. It also meant going to play what they call outings, where John and sometimes other celebrities would play golf with the company's bigwigs and important clients, usually for a fee. John even got hired sometimes to do outings for companies that weren't his sponsors. A lot of time in between tournaments was spent being flown around to these outings on the companies' private jets. He usually made $50,000 to $100,000 per appearance, so it was a good gig for an afternoon's work. Many times I would get to go with him and spend the day at the event, or I would go shopping if one of the other wives was there too.

During that first year, John was flown to Canada to do an outing for Magna International. I think they were the richest group of people I've ever seen in my life. Everything was just gorgeous and over the top. The other celebrities were a couple of stars from *90210* and Bill Clinton. It was a great, fun day. I was walking the course with them, watching them play, and Clinton was just taking mulligan after mulligan. (That's what they call a do-over. See, I couldn't help but learn a few things about golf, even though I'm still far from a fan.) We were all laughing and enjoying ourselves. Everything went smoothly until dinner. The company founder's daughter was hosting the event, and she had told me that it was casual dress, and I should wear what I had on that day. Well, I was wearing my usual fat pants and tank top, and I had been rained on at the golf course, so my hair was half curly, half straight, and I looked like a mess pot with flip-flops. That would have been bad enough, but when we got to the dinner spot, the place was super fancy, with these ice sculptures everywhere, and it was completely semiformal cocktail attire. Now, John could have cared less that he was wearing jeans and a T-shirt. He would always not dress accordingly. I think I only saw him in a tie once the whole time we were married, and that wasn't even on our wedding day. But I would have dressed the right way if they had given me a clue. I was so embarrassed, especially when they sat me at the main table. There I was, looking like a wet little dog, sitting with all of the government people and Bill Clinton. But I made the best of it, as I always do. I started chugging beers and talking to this lady who had been involved in some big scandal because of an affair she'd had or something. So at least that made me feel a little better about myself, and I ended up forgetting about how I looked and enjoyed myself.

When it was time to fly back to the States, they had a private plane for Clinton and John. Clinton's people were in charge of who sat where, and someone put me in the front right beside Clinton. John was way in back. Well, John was not happy about that. He's from Arkansas, and he's always been a Clinton fan. Not to mention the fact that he's insanely jealous. Ever since that night, John would not even take a call from Bill Clinton.

Well, I had never thought much about Clinton one way or the other. But it was a long flight from Canada to Las Vegas, and I'd had enough beers, so we started talking. He was reading a *LIFE* magazine article about stem cell research.

"What do you think about that?" I asked, peering over his shoulder.

I'd only heard the Baptist and Republican versions of the whole stem cell debate, and so I'd always thought it was a bunch of scientists who secretly wanted to do cloning, and that it was sacrilegious.

Well, by the time Bill Clinton had explained it to me, he was so brilliant and such a good talker that I was totally for it.

I completely loved him to death. And no, he wasn't suggestive to me, or anything like that, no matter how jealous John made himself. Clinton was just so nice, and such a genuine person. I could tell that he actually listened to everyone, even the wet dog at the party. So I'll always be a big, huge Bill Clinton fan.

That was one of the first times I saw John's jealous side, which got a lot worse as time went on, and I think his own guilty conscience started to bother him more and more. But things were fairly quiet, especially compared to how they later got. The only bad thing was that as soon as the sponsors and money came back, so did all of the hangers-on. They just swarmed John, and they did not care about getting along with his wife or his family. In fact, they were happy if they could get us into a fight, because then I'd be left at home, and they'd get to be out and about alone with the star, gaining backstage access to concerts and generally being in the middle of everything. Many of these people caused John—and myself—so many problems.

When we were traveling, it was okay. John was a normal, nice husband, and our life together worked. Back in Memphis, we usually stayed at my parents' house because John had sold his house at Southwind, and we hadn't had the chance to buy a new one yet. But John was always hell-bent on getting himself to Arkansas. As soon as we crossed the state line, he'd drop Austin and me off and get up to no good. He'd head right to the casino, holing up for two days and nights, and I never knew if he was going to come back with a lot of money or broke. Or he'd go off and drink and party, and just be a disaster. He'd be hanging out with his brother and all of his old buddies, and all they did was drink. They'd go over to John's house at seven or eight in the morning, dragging these huge coolers of beer that were half as big as a bed, and all of them would drink like forty beers in a day. It was like a fraternity party or something I've never even seen before. And I'm a drinker. I like to drink. So it takes a lot to shock me. The worst part of it was that when he was up there, he didn't answer the telephone for days. As I soon learned, that was one of his things. John disappeared a lot.

John's best friend, Donnie, who was one of the worst hangers-on until John finally fired him years later, could not stand me from the day John and I got married. For one thing, I thought it was ridiculous for John to pay him $100,000 a year to drive the bus, when professional bus drivers only made $50,000 and John did most of the driving anyway. And I thought it was *totally* crazy that Donnie lived in the Arkansas house with us, even after we got married. I mean, how old were we?

I wasn't the only one who didn't understand the arrangement, either. I remember going over to have a glass of wine with John's mom, Lou, one night. Her house was right through our back gate, and we liked to get together and talk.

"When are you going to ask Donnie to move out?" she asked. "Doesn't it kind of bother you that you can't even walk through your own house naked?"

"Lou, I've got to pick my battles," I said.

And I did. I was unimpressed with the way John's two daughters were taken care of, especially since he paid approximately $10,000 a month in child support for each of those kids, and the youngest child would show up for visits at his house in ratty clothes. I didn't care about the money. I always felt like they were his kids, and so they should have it. But I didn't want to be seen around Memphis with them looking like Raggedy Ann dolls, especially with us having so much, so I tried to make sure they had everything they needed.

That was my thing in general, especially when my life with John started to go bad. I wanted everything to look pretty. The first thing I tackled was the house in Arkansas. It had hope but it needed help. I remember the first time he brought me there, I was like, okay, you made millions and millions of dollars and you have dirty, metal miniblinds in here. John was always very clean, but the house was a mess. The Berber carpet had stains. I thought it was horrible and asked him if I could redecorate. I figured he'd just won after six years of losing, I'd seen him spend $500,000 in one night at the casino, so I could spend $100,000 on the house. John let me go ahead and do whatever I wanted. I will give him that: He could be incredibly generous, and he did provide very well for Austin and me back then.

John and I were in Germany for the BMW International when the decorators got started. They made some decorative changes to the house and brought over potential furniture, and then I was going to decide what I liked when we got back. But when we returned home and saw what had been done, we discovered that a small mishap had occurred.

It was far from a big mistake, but it was a big moment in our marriage. John and I walked into the house with Lou Daly and a few of our neighbors. We were chitchatting, talking about our trip to Europe and what we were planning to do to the house. I was explaining my plans for redecorating and taking them through the rooms, showing them how everything was going to look when it was done. Well, we got as far as the kitchen, and that's when I saw a side of John I'd never seen before. The decorators had accidentally brought some wrong paint with them, and the walls were a light green tone instead of the earthy brown color I had picked out.

So, in front of everyone, in front of his own mother, John whipped it out and started peeing all over the wall.

"This is what I think about this color," he said.

We all just stood there and watched him. I did not know what to say. I think I was in shock. I was saying plenty inside my head though, like: *Oh my God, what have I done? Who have I married? And what am I going to do? I mean, what grown man would have his penis out in front of his mother?*

This was the exact moment when I officially knew that I was in for it. Up until then, it had always bugged me that no one took our marriage seriously. Not only did they claim I was only in it for the money, but they said it was doomed from the start. I wouldn't say I'm a real prideful person, but I've got a strong will. And when everyone predicted that we wouldn't be married for six months, I always felt like I had to prove them wrong. Well, right then, I saw exactly how challenging that might be.

That was basically my official welcome to Arkansas. Because it never got any better than that, and it often got a whole lot worse when we were there. His friends thought it was funny to egg him on and get him to drink whiskey, which just made him so stupid. Like when he pissed on the wall that day, that was just him getting warmed up. When John was drunk on whiskey, he would go into this blind rage, where he completely lost it. I always said there were three Johns. There was the John who I married: He was cool, and we might have a few differences, but we'd always get along okay. There was Johnny: He came out after John had been really drunk and bad sometimes, and he was almost like this baby who would literally get into a fetal position on the floor, and I felt sorry for him because he was totally at my mercy. And then there was JD: He was possessed by a demon, and over the years he spit in my face, nearly burnt my house down, and told my niece that her mother was a whore.

Well, on this particular evening in Arkansas, we were dealing with JD.

Later that night, he destroyed all of the new stuff that the decorator had brought. He took the lamps and shattered them. He broke up all of the family pictures. There was this antique china cabinet against one wall, and he busted all the windows out of it. I think it ended up being like $30,000 worth of stuff. They had brought extra pieces to show me how they would look in the house, and I hadn't decided if I was going to buy them yet or not. Well, John decided that for me real quick. He smashed everything to bits, and just like that, I had bought the whole lot of them.

I couldn't believe it. I just *could not believe it*. Like I said, I'd heard that he'd been wild when he was younger, and I knew that he'd gotten into trouble for smashing up hotel rooms and a couple of houses when he lived with his ex-wives. But I'd never seen it before. I'd thought all of that was behind him. And besides, I don't think I really understood how bad he could get. It's one thing to hear about someone trashing a TV or breaking a window; it's another thing to have your entire house torn down around you by a total and complete maniac who's supposed to be your husband. This was one of so many moments in my marriage when I found myself thinking: *Is this really happening? This cannot be real.* It would either be so amazingly good it couldn't possibly be real, like having a million dollars on the bed when we got married; or it'd be so incredibly awful that I was wishing it wasn't real, like this time in Arkansas, and more moments than I can count after it.

In the morning, his friends came and cleaned everything up, John paid for the furniture, and it really was like it had never happened. If there was any noticeable difference afterward, it was only that John was very sorry and extra sweet with me, which did go far toward making me less angry. So I put it behind me, and I assumed life would go back to normal. I guess that depends on your definition of "normal."

three

A SON FOR THE KING

Now, like I said right from the start, if I'm going to tell on John, I've got to tell on myself too. I'm not completely innocent. I like to drink, and sometimes I can get a little wild. This was especially true when I was married to John, and he would start in on me like he sometimes did when he had been drinking. He had this way of pushing me until I finally snapped and pushed back. Eventually, I had to stop drinking around him because I came to realize that being sober was the only way I could be sure to keep my cool and also try to keep him from destroying things too badly. But early in our marriage, it could get pretty insane.

This one time, it was near when we first got married, we went to a football game at the University of Arkansas, which is where John had gone to college, and so he was a huge Razorbacks fan. Well, I had been drinking PGA punch—as in Pure Grain Alcohol punch—with the cheerleaders while we were there, so I was already feeling a little saucy when it was time to go home. We got on the bus and drove back to Memphis with Darius Rucker and his band-mates from Hootie & the Blowfish, who had been at the game with us too. John wasn't driving that day, and so we were all drinking and partying and having a good time. I know I had definitely had a few beers. And then, John crossed that line where he wasn't fun drunk anymore, and he was moving into JD territory fast. I can't even re-member what it was that set him off, not that it had to be anything more than some notion in his head that I was being a stupid cunt, as he liked to call me when he was drunk and belligerent. He started yelling at me, and then he pointed his finger at me. Well, you can-not stick your finger in my face because that turns me into a crazy person. So that's the first thing: Don't point at me. Ever. Just don't do it. Then, here's another: Respect my personal space. Don't get in it, unless you're going to kiss me, and I want you to. Well, he wasn't about to kiss me, and even if he had been, I certainly didn't want him to right then. Finally, he crossed the limit. We were standing real close to each other in the bus's kitchen, which wasn't a big space to begin with, and what with all the yelling he was doing, he spit in my face. That finally put me over the edge.

I pushed him to get him out of my face, and he lost his balance. There was a cooler behind him, and he stumbled against it and fell backward onto the floor. I'm sure it looked like I was a superhuman to be able to knock down such a big guy. But, really, it was just one of those accidents that happen. And then he said I punched him in the lip. I have to confess that this was another one of those moments when I blacked out, even though I'm not proud to admit it, and I can tell you that I never drank PGA punch again after that day. So I cannot confirm or deny clocking him. I simply can't remember either way. But a couple of months after that, I did ask Darius about it.

"You know when me and John got into it on the bus, did I, um, did I punch him?" I asked.

"You did," he said. "After you pushed him, you tagged him two times on the way down."

Now, Darius wouldn't lie. So I must have hit John, even if I can't remember it. Not that I'm surprised that I did. He was being very in my face, and like anyone else, I have my breaking point. That doesn't mean I think it's a good way to behave, though. We didn't normally go around hitting each other. And I started trying to be more careful about not letting him push me so far after that. Sometimes it just got a little out of control. Well, more often than not, when it came to the two of us, it got *a lot* out of control in later years, but we weren't there yet.

And we had bigger things to worry about soon after that. In February 2002, we were in San Diego for a tournament. We had some time off, so we were just walking around, sightseeing and shopping. My phone rang, and it was my mom.

"Sherrie," she said. "I don't know what's going on, but the feds came to our house, and they're just taking apart everything, and your dad told me not to come home. I'm at Macy's buying perfume. I don't know what I'm doing."

Now, this had been brewing for a while, but we hadn't thought anything would come of it. A few months before, some of my dad's friends had been investigated for supposedly dealing drugs and then laundering the money. These were nice people: guys at Arkansas State, guys who had legitimate businesses, guys who went to church every Sunday. Now, their businesses—a pallet company, a drag strip, and nightclubs—were all businesses that dealt in a lot of cash, but we'd never had any reason to think anything of it. And we couldn't believe that they'd done anything wrong. Even harder to fathom was that, suddenly, my dad was being investigated because he had sold these guys some cars and loaned them money over the years.

This was an incredibly upsetting time for my family, dealing with lawyers and court dates and worrying that my dad might go to jail, or even that my mom and I might get in trouble too, because we had both handled money for him at his car lot. Well, John actually did something for my dad during this whole nightmare that showed off the sweet side that had made me fall in love with him in the first place, and that could maybe provide an answer for anyone who's thinking: *Okay, dum-dum, why'd you stay with that psycho son of a bitch for all those years?*

It all started with my brother going out one night—we won't say if he was drunk or not, we'll just assume he was drunk—and while he was driving home, he wrecked my dad's brand-new truck. He basically split it down the middle. Now, my parents were already under a lot of stress, and we didn't have hold of a lot of money, so this was the worst time to buy a new truck. Well, John had just purchased a truck from the local Chevrolet dealer to do maintenance for one of the businesses he owned, and just like that, he took my dad right back over there and bought my dad a brand-new truck. John paid for the whole thing up front and gave my dad the title. I mean, my dad was nearly in tears. And he is an old school Southern gentleman. He does *not* make a fuss. But he had worked hard for every dime he'd ever spent, and he'd been a giver his whole life. No one had ever done anything like that for him before. And it deeply moved him. He always thought of John like a son. Of course, that only made it harder later on.

John and I actually did all sorts of little sweet things for each other in the beginning. He knew that I loved those mini Reese's Peanut Butter Cups, and he would always buy them for me and line them up on my pillow so they spelled *I love you*. And because I felt so bad about how calloused his hands and feet were from playing so much golf, I'd give him manicures and pedicures when we had downtime on the bus and we were just hanging out together, watching movies. It could be real nice and normal.

Not that life with John could ever be counted on to be peaceful for very long, even during what were the good years. Especially when it came to Arkansas. Something about being in his old hometown of Dardanelle was always a nightmare for me. And what was even worse than a regular day in Dardanelle was the way John behaved at his annual charity event for the Boys and Girls Clubs. I don't know what it was about that weekend, but it just brought out the worst in him. It was always held around Memorial Day, and so the first time I went, we had been married for about a year. I thought it was going to be a nice weekend away in the country, so I invited my family and a bunch of our friends and neighbors up from Memphis, which meant that there were more witnesses present for the carnage that was about to go down.

As was often the case, the problems started with John's bud-dies, which meant they started with drinking. Those hillbilly trolls came over to the house first thing in the morning with one of those big coolers they were always dragging around, just crammed with beer. And they would go through it too. I swear, John would drink upward of sixty beers in a day. Throw in some whiskey, and it was pretty much guaranteed that JD would show up for a visit before the day was over.

When he was drinking at his charity event, John always seemed to forget that he was married, which goes to show how bombed he was, since this was the one happening that was held at the house he shared with his *wife*. That first year I was busy being the hostess and getting used to how John usually did things. And then I looked out on the porch at some point during the afternoon and saw John dancing with some woman, and not in a friendly way, either. They were slow dancing, and they were all over each other. Now, this was at my house, and there were hundreds of people there in my backyard—guests that we had invited, including people from the Boys and Girls Clubs—so I tried to keep my cool.

I walked out onto the porch and went over to them as quietly as possible, so as not to draw further attention to what was going on. John and the woman didn't even look up when I approached. They were in their own little world.

I tapped the woman on her shoulder.

"Look, this is all cool and everything when I'm not around," I said. "But my friends are here, and you're being quite embar-rassing."

Now, I wasn't really cool with it, of course. And John knew that, no matter how blotto he was. I was mad, and hurt, and I felt humiliated because he had behaved like this in front of everyone who was there. But I didn't say anything more about my feelings. I just went inside and got myself ready to leave, so I wouldn't lose it and make a big, nasty scene. Well, I guess I shouldn't have worried about that. As usual, John took care of making a scene.

As soon as I walked away from him, he let go of the girl, and he just lost his mind. Our first bus was parked out in back of the house, and he climbed aboard it and started throwing things through all of the windows. I was standing in the driveway, and these explosions of glass were flying all over the ground. My friend Angela's husband, Brett, leaned in the open door and tried to talk some sense into the maniac.

"John?" he said.

BAM! was the answer he got, as an ashtray John had thrown at him hit the door near his head.

"Okay, I just dodged an ashtray," he said, and he backed his way down off the bus. Shortest intervention ever.

John kept smashing everything he could get his hands on. He even tried to set the bus on fire. John has always been a heavy smoker, and he liked to light his cigarettes with one of those Zippo lighters, which has a wick and butane, so he always had lighter fluid around. He was going nuts, squirting fluid everywhere inside the bus. Luckily he didn't get a fire going, but he probably couldn't have done much more damage if he had burned the whole thing down to the ground. As it was, he didn't stop until he had pretty much destroyed the entire inside of that bus.

So then he stumbled off the bus and out into the driveway. He saw me standing there, and he started cursing me out right in front of everyone. Next he went to the garage and set in on my car. Now, this was a very nice car: a Mercedes S65, four-door sedan that was probably worth $140,000. Not for long. I don't even know how he picked it up, but he grabbed one of these four-foot-tall urn-shaped plant stands we had, and he started beating up my car so bad. It was a massacre. He knocked out all of the windows and put dents in it everywhere. I couldn't even believe what I was seeing.

Or hearing: He kept on cussing me the whole time he was going nuts.

Oh God, I thought. *What am I going to do?*

Well, what I did is what I soon learned that everyone always did for John. I helped him clean up his mess and cover up his craziness. When there was nothing left to smash outside, he went into the house. He was running through the back of the house, tearing everything down from the walls—pictures and shelves and whatever else he could get his hands on. People were getting out of his way, and there was nothing that could stop him until he finally tripped and fell down. So he was lying there in the midst of all this chaos he had caused, and he was so worked up that I guess his buddies thought he was having a heart attack. His chest was heaving. He couldn't breathe. He pretty much passed out cold. They called an ambulance, and it came screaming up to the house with its sirens on. Mind you, this was still in the middle of the party, and we had guests everywhere in the yard.

I was still acting like the good little wife, covering for him the whole time, trying to pretend like nothing was going on and making sure everyone was having a nice time. When the ambulance arrived, I went back to where they were loading him onto a stretcher to make sure he was okay. He was real drunk and out of it. And even though he had been so bad to me, cussing me out and everything, I thought, *I'm his wife. I guess I'm supposed to go with him to the hospital.*

So I went along in the ambulance, even though I probably shouldn't have, since it made it seem like he could do whatever he wanted and get away with it. As far as he and his people were concerned, he could. They came up with this story, and I told the press that John had taken so much Dexatrim that day that it had sped his heart up and made him pass out, or something like that. It all got blamed on Dexatrim, and I felt so bad for them. Here we were, killing this company, when John was the one who had probably drank something like a hundred beers. I felt like saying, *Yeah, I don't think the makers of Dexatrim would recommend that anyone use their product while consuming fifty or sixty beers. I'd think anyone might have a few side effects after that.*

This was one of the first times that I saw his agent Bud Martin in action, and I couldn't believe how he and everyone was covering up for John, just like it was nothing. But I became real familiar with that kind of thing in the years to come. It wasn't just Bud, either. The PGA, the media, everyone we came across seemed to have a way of making anything bad that John did go away. And, of course, I did too, back then. Bud called John "the King," and in the beginning, John used to call me "Queenie," and when he would buy me presents, which he loved to do—especially clothes; believe it or not, that man had a knack for picking out women's fashions— he'd always say, "It's for the Queen." Well, I liked the sound of that, all right. I think every wife wants to be a Queen. The problem is that it wasn't easy to stay on the King's good side, and then it was peasant time.

That summer was a real rocky time for our whole family. Not only were my parents going through their court proceedings, but we had some rough spells with his family too. At this one particular family party in Arkansas on the Fourth of July, I got an idea of how John had inherited some of his bad habits. Now, the whole day was off-the-charts crazy to begin with. I swear there was something wrong with that house. While the kids were in the back bedroom having their nap, the wiring for the surround sound overheated and started a fire. We were able to put it out, but it was scary, especially because John and all his trolls were already running around drunk by the time it happened. And the next morning, we woke up to find that the English bulldog, Wrinkles, which John had bought for the kids had drowned in the pool. But that's not even the worst of what happened. The night of the party, the kids and I were asleep on the bus because we had so many guests staying in the house, when the bus door rang, and my friend Kelly was standing outside. Now, John's dad had been following her around all night, drunk, and hitting on her to the point where it wasn't quite right, but we kind of let it go because we figured he was the dad. But, finally, he had gotten way out of control drunk, and she was worried.

I went back into the house, and John's dad could barely stand up on his own two feet. He was slurring and stumbling, and just a total mess. John and his brother had been drinking pretty hard all day too, so they weren't looking much better. There was definitely a family resemblance. Anyhow, I went with John and his brother to walk their dad home. Even though their house was right behind our backyard, this took some doing. Finally, I was in John's parents' bedroom, trying to get his dad into bed. Well, I guess he decided he wasn't ready to go to bed, because he leaned over its side, and when he came back up there was something in his hand.

"That's a fucking gun!" I said.

I got out of his way real fast and started yelling for John and his brother.

"Y'all, he's got a gun!" I said. "He's got a gun!"

Well, he staggered out of the bedroom and into the living room where John and his brother were. He raised that gun up and pointed it at John, and then he swung and pointed it at his brother. It was this weird, unbelievable moment, like something from a movie. And then, real quick, his brother slapped the gun out of his dad's hand and got a hold of it. In all of the confusion, the gun went off. I was so scared. I thought for sure he had shot his dad. They finally managed to calm him down and get him to bed. I don't think his dad even remembered it in the morning. But he did start AA, and he never drank again. Right after that whole ordeal, Lou was going to divorce his dad, but they decided to stay together and work it out.

And then Lou got sick. She was diagnosed with lung cancer that summer. She didn't do chemo or radiation; they found an experimental place for her in Vegas, but it wasn't enough, and her health deteriorated almost immediately. John was incredibly close with his mom, and I know it broke him up inside when she got sick. But, like a lot of men, he did *not* talk about his feelings, and he couldn't deal with it at all. He wouldn't even go see her. I think it was too hard for him.

That fall, we traveled overseas quite a bit. While we were in Australia in November, I found out that I was pregnant, which we could not have been happier about. John loved his two daughters, and he was a devoted stepfather to my son, Austin, but like a lot of men he really wanted a son of his own. And so we had been trying for two months, and I had been reading all of these books about all of the tricks there were for making sure the King got his boy-child, doing it doggy-style and on certain days of the month. And finally, it had happened. While the baby was a blessing, and the absolute best thing that came out of my marriage, it also complicated things because it gave me another reason—the strongest argument of all, really—to want to stay with John and keep our family together, no matter how bad he behaved. Even though Austin was growing up into the sweetest kid with almost no input from his dad, I've always believed it's best for kids to be raised by both parents, and so I did my best to stick by John. And that made my life a whole lot harder, given what was about to happen next. The same day we found out about the baby, and we were so happy and enjoying all of these wonderful things that were happening, like the nice little speech that Greg Norman made at dinner that night, congratulating us, we also got the call that Lou Daly had passed away. John was shattered.

But he wouldn't admit it. We were back in the hotel room after dinner, and I was trying to comfort him, but he wouldn't even let me do that.

"Let's get on a plane," I said. "Let's go home."

"No, my mom would want me to play," he said.

As usual, I didn't say anything to contradict him, and I went along with what he wanted. But I was real worried, because he was acting like a zombie. It was like he wouldn't even acknowledge it. We stayed a whole week. And then, at the end of that week, he decided to stay another week and go to a different tournament. They kept her, I guess, in the morgue refrigerator for two weeks. I couldn't believe it. That didn't seem like any way to honor the mother he loved so much. Now, he said he was playing for his mother, but he had no business being out there just then. I've seen a lot of bad behavior from John Daly over the years, but I have never seen him be such a poor sport on a golf course as he was during that period.

First of all, he never really tried the whole time that he was playing. He swatted the ball all over the place. And then, finally, it was like he couldn't even hold it together well enough to do that little. So he threw his putter up in the air, and it fell into the water, and he walked off the greens and away from the course without saying anything to anyone. He didn't go sign his score-card, which all of the players are required to do; otherwise, they are disqualified.

Now, I had no idea that any of this had happened. I made sure to be at the scoring tent when he should have been there, just like I always did, because I knew he had a way of leaving immediately after he had finished the eighteenth hole, and I didn't want to get left behind. So I ran around to where his cart was supposed to be, and I sat down and I waited. And I waited. And I waited. Finally, an hour went by and I was wondering where he was. But there was still no John. So I was standing there like I was stupid or something, because I had no idea what to do. I didn't even know how to get back to where we were staying. Here we were, all the way around the world in Australia, I'd just found out I was pregnant, and I had no idea where my husband was or what kind of state he'd be in when I found him.

Finally, this nice man who worked for the tournament came over to me.

"Mrs. Daly, I think John walked back to his accommodations," he said. "Do you need a ride?"

"I guess so," I said, feeling like a moron because of John once again.

I wasn't the only one who felt like John had no business being out on a golf course when he was that much of a mess. When we were back at our rental house that night, John's agent told us that Greg Norman had said John was an insult to the game. It was hard not to agree. There was one appearance he made while we were down there, for which I think they paid him a fee of somewhere between $200,000 and $500,000—and golf is not a big sport in Australia, so that was a lot of money for them to come up with just because they had so much respect and admiration for John. Well, he put an end to that; it was pretty much the same nonsense that whole day too. The whole thing was hard to watch.

And of course John never apologized or bothered to explain himself for any of it. I wasn't mad at him right then because I knew how devastated he was about his mom. But I still didn't like being treated like that. And besides, that was the only time he had a reasonable excuse. And he used to do stuff like that all the time. If he got mad at a golf tournament, if I wasn't at the car, he would go into fits and drive off and leave me, and I would have to catch a ride with the courtesy car or figure something else out. It could be pretty embarrassing to be Mrs. John Daly.

When we finally got home from Australia two weeks later, it was the strangest thing ever. Usually people are beside themselves when a loved one has died. Not the Daly family. No one was crying or acting upset. They all started drinking and partying, except for John's dad, who was still in AA. And I know that people do that too, when that's the only way they can seem to dull the pain. But still, the whole thing was so weird to me. I think it would have been good if John could have cried. It sure would have been a lot healthier for him, and a lot better for our marriage. But after that, he just started partying a lot. And he started trying to hide his bad behavior from me too, which is actually so much worse than having it out in the open.

I can still remember, right around that time, I was walking through the house, and I had this habit of grabbing his drink to get a sip out of it. He always had a Diet Coke around somewhere, because he was the same way with soda as he was with everything else—cigarettes, booze, sex: He couldn't get enough, and he would usually drink something like twenty-four Diet Cokes in a day. Well, I took a big gulp and my throat started burning and my eyes started watering. It had whiskey in it. And the way I felt, I was just crushed. Like, instead of my eyes welling up with tears, my whole body welled up. It was one thing when he was drinking whiskey at parties because he'd already had a few beers (or a few dozen) and his judgment wasn't working right. But for him to be drinking whiskey around the house like that, when he was the one who had warned me how bad it made him act—even told me to leave him if I ever caught him with it—well, I knew right then: *Here we go. If he's started this, we're done.* But of course, I stuck around just to be sure.

four

LIFE ON THE DRUNK BUS

MAYBE JOHN HAD ALWAYS LIED and I'd been too in love with him, and too naive in general, to pick up on it. Given everything that came out by the end, it's hard to imagine a time when he wasn't cutting up and then covering it up, although I'd still like to think we were as happy as I felt like we were in the beginning. Either way, once I caught John lying, it seemed like all he did was tell fibs. And he wasn't very good at it, either. So I was always catching him at something or other.

I caught the first lie about something he was getting up to

with his buddies in January of 2003. We were out in Ontario, California, for a tournament. And we were visiting our good friends Mark and Mary Ellen Leggio. The business Mark owns with his brother Chris, Mark Christopher Chevrolet, sponsors John. And Mary Ellen quickly became one of my best girlfriends. We spent a lot of time with them during those years, and they are the godparents of both Austin and Little John. Well, John told me that he and his friends and a bunch of other guys were going to go down to this bar to watch sumo wrestlers, or some other kind of big fat wrestlers or boxers or something. Obviously, I had no desire to see anything nasty like that, so I stayed behind. Later, I casually mentioned to Mary Ellen what the guys were doing.

"Sumo?" she said. "That's not right. It's college girls boxing night."

Since her husband owned an interest in the place, I figured she ought to know.

"I'm calling up there," I said.

We called the bar, and sure enough it was college girls boxing night. The only thing big and fat going on was John's lie.

Determined to bust him, I got Mary Ellen to watch Austin for me and I drove over to the bar.

And there was John, like a big pervert, sitting ringside with all of his friends. And these college girls were all half-naked, with these big blown-up boxing gloves on their hands, just bouncing around and being a spectacle.

I was so mad at the deception that I took John's cap off and popped him in the back of his head with it.

"You want to see boxing?" I said to John and his entourage.

"Pick anyone out of here and I'll kick their ass. And I'll tell all your wives that you're here too."

John didn't get why I was so mad, but to me, the scene felt akin to a strip club. Plus, he had *lied* about it. That's what hurt most. And then he refused to leave with me, even though he knew how angry I was. It was like my happiness meant nothing to him.

I went back alone to where we had the bus parked at Mark and Mary Ellen's house, and I packed up all of my things. I got myself an airline ticket to leave the next day for Memphis. When I got to the airport in the morning, I wasn't feeling well at all. I started feeling really dizzy, and I got worried because I was a few months pregnant, and I thought I was having a miscarriage. Plus, I had Austin with me, and I didn't want to scare him, but I couldn't leave him alone either. I found this couple in the waiting area who looked like they were nice people.

"Ma'am, can you please help me to the bathroom," I said. "I think I'm about to pass out."

She rushed over and started to help lead me toward the ladies' room.

"And can your husband watch my little boy?" I said.

I was so embarrassed. I had this perfect stranger helping me put wet paper towels on my head because I had broken out in this cold, crazy sweat.

I really thought something was wrong with the baby, and so I ended up calling John and having him come get us. Luckily, everything was fine, at least with my pregnancy. And John apologized his way out of it. Again. And because of the baby on the way, I stayed. Again. That was definitely a theme that year.

If life on the road had once been fairly quiet, then things went nuts when we got home, especially when John was in Arkansas with the trolls. The fact that things were now wild on the road meant that life at home was even more out of control. Even when things started out as a quiet family dinner, there was no telling how they'd end up. During one of our breaks from the road, John was hanging out a lot with his Arkansas buddies. They were all planning to spend the day over at the golf course near our house, and John was in a particularly good mood.

Before he left, John had a request for me.

"Would you cook your spaghetti for dinner tonight?" he said.

John loved my spaghetti, and I was happy to make him happy.

"How many people?" I said.

"Well, the guys are coming over."

So I cooked spaghetti for around fifteen people. It was even more than that, actually. It was enough for fifteen grownups, plus whatever kids were around. I got everything ready—the spaghetti, the bread, the whole deal—and dinnertime came and went, but they didn't show up. I called John's phone. No answer.

My sister-in-law and I were sitting there, waiting. And all of the kids were complaining that they were hungry and asking if they could start eating.

"No, you can't eat," we said. "We're waiting."

Because of course I wanted to set up the table so it looked pretty and have everyone eating together. So I wouldn't let anyone touch anything.

An hour went by. Still, nobody was answering their phones: not John, and not his brother either.

Another hour passed.

I finally admitted that we were not going to have the respectable family dinner that I had hoped to enjoy. I gave the kids their dinner and put them to bed.

Midnight came and went, and he still didn't come home.

So by then, I was furious. And I wanted him to know it.

For some reason, he had put this carpet in the garage, which I thought was stupid to begin with, so I took the huge pot of uneaten spaghetti out there, and I dumped it all over that rug. It was a lot of spaghetti, and it went everywhere. Then I put two Diet Coke cans out beside it, and I stuck a butcher knife into each of the Coke cans for emphasis and lit candles, so they would be all burned to stubs. I wanted to create a psycho-looking scene.

He didn't come home all night, and so I got wilder and wilder. In the morning, I called my sister-in-law and told her to come back over. I was looking for any way I could to make the point that I would not be treated like this.

John had this big stuffed hog at the house because he was such a fan of those University of Arkansas Razorbacks. It was big and ugly, and I hated it as much as he loved it. In other words, it was the perfect target.

"Help me pull this hog into the driveway," I said, trying to drag it out.

I wanted him to run over it when he pulled into the driveway.

But it was too heavy, even with the maid helping us.

So then I was even more riled up. My revenge plan hadn't worked out, and I still hadn't heard from him. My next idea was to take all of these signed jerseys John had framed in the house and spread them out flat on the driveway, so that when he drove up he would run over the top of them. But just about that time he saved himself, because he pulled in before I could get them all laid out.

I had been all worked up, but when he finally came home, I just stood there. It was like I would get so sick of being ignored like that—whether for twenty-four hours or several days—but then, by the time I had sat there that whole time, alone and crying, I didn't even have the energy left to be mad.

He didn't apologize. But he did take notice of the spaghetti. I think he even called over to his brother's house about it.

"Oh, my God, she's crazy," he said. "You should see this. I'm coming over."

That was fine by me. I wanted him to think I was crazy. Whether it's right or wrong, I was trying to put the fear of God in him. I wanted to send him the message: *You don't come home to me until a day later, after I cooked spaghetti for fifteen people because you asked all nice.*

I did want to create a real freaky scene in the garage, and I succeeded, if I do say so myself. A lot of people would probably say that's insane. Fine, let them. My sister-in-law and I laughed about it all night, and that was a lot better than all the nights I spent crying because of things John did and said. I was so sad at being treated like that by my husband, especially when we were starting a family and supposed to be happy.

"How could you do this to me?" I would always say.

But he never had a good answer, or much of an answer at all.

I fought back because I realized that I had to make men think I was crazy for them to take me seriously. The nice voice had gotten me nowhere.

I was becoming increasingly devastated that my marriage wasn't the happy, quiet life that I'd thought I was getting with

John. I would have given anything if ugly collared shirts were my biggest source of bother. By now I'd spent enough time on the PGA Tour to realize how wrong I'd been when I'd worried that everyone in the golf world was so perfect and preppy and well behaved compared to John and me.

Only I wasn't ready to admit how deep the problems went. I still wanted to hold it together for our family. And for John. I had loved him too much for too long to not care that he was so torn up about losing his mom. Even when he was wasted, it made me sad, because he was so pathetic, almost like this retarded little boy. And I'm not using that word as an insult, either. I mean, like a real mentally handicapped person, because he certainly wasn't a grown man who had all of his wits about him when he was misbehaving. So, because I felt sorry for him, and I was in denial about what was really going on in our marriage, I was still lying for him. In fact, that stripper story at the Make-A-Wish benefit had a whole second act that's still hard for me to tell, because it really shows John at his worst, and I was so used to hiding it from people for so long. But I did say right up front that I was going to let it rip.

Not too long after the spaghetti mess was the incident with the strippers. If I seemed insane, jumping off golf carts and choking and punching people, maybe it's a little easier to understand why, now. I probably was insane, at least a little bit. I was eight months pregnant, so my hormones were all over the place. I was fed up with John for being drunk and mean and cussing me out all of the time. And I was deeply embarrassed at how often he did it in front of other people.

So, on that day at the Make-A-Wish benefit, after I had choked the stripper and punched our banker, after John had hit me in my pregnant belly with a beer bottle and left me standing there in front of everyone, I didn't leave like I probably should have. I went to find him. I got someone with a golf cart to drop me off at our bus. Only John wouldn't let me on. Donnie Crabtree was behind the wheel and—no surprise here—he actually tried to drive away. Well, I was still worked up from earlier, and I wasn't about to get left behind on top of everything else. So I got right in front of that bus, and I just stood there. Donnie wasn't about to run over a pregnant lady—I'm sure he thought about it, though—so he managed to control himself and stopped right in front of me. They finally opened the door and let me on. The bus was crowded with a whole bunch of people—John, Donnie, and three other guys and a girl—and they were still partying. I was not in the mood.

I turned and headed toward the bedroom at the back of the bus. But John was really, really drunk—whiskey drunk—and all worked up.

"Get out of here," John said, coming after me.

"You're not leaving me here," I said, turning back to face off against him. "I don't even have a way home."

He lost it then, like I'd seen him do so many times before. Only this time, it was directed at me. He reached behind him and picked up this fruitcake that was sitting on the kitchen counter. He came after me with it, and I was so surprised that I didn't even try to get out of the way. But then, when I realized he was really going to do it, it was too late. He was big and drunk and heated, and he trapped me in that little narrow hallway and smushed the whole cake in my face and all over my hair. He was so much bigger than me that, as he did it, he knocked me down on the floor with how hard he was pressing that cake into my face. Now, mind you, I was pregnant, and there were all of these grown men standing there. But no one defended me. No one told him to stop. They were too busy kissing up to him, so they'd be the ones who got to hang out and party with John, and be backstage, and all of that stuff that goes along with celebrity. By that point, I was hysterical, yelling and crying at John and trying to get him to stop. It didn't help that I was having trouble getting up because my belly was so big and fat, and it was slippery from the cake that was smeared everywhere.

John kept right at me, and now I was getting scared. I knew there was no talking sense to him when he was in a state like this, and that he could go on for a long time and break a lot of stuff while he was at it. He kicked at the part of the cake that he hadn't already broken and smushed that into my face too, and then he started smacking me in the back of the head. I was really crying then, and there was cake all over my face, and I was a total mess. And still, no one came over to help me or even suggested to John that maybe this wasn't a good way to be treating his pregnant wife. While all of this was going on, Donnie started driving the bus away from the country club, so now I was trapped with these people.

And then, just like that, John stopped and went back to the party at the front of the bus. I got myself up off the floor, but I was still shaking and crying. Before I had a chance to calm down or get myself cleaned up, even a little bit, John had Donnie pull over a few miles down the road, and he dragged me off the bus and put me out on the side of Interstate 40. As I watched the bus drive away, I was standing there, crying and crying and crying. I had cake all up in my face and my hair, and I didn't know what to do. I didn't want my parents to know that John had done this to me. So I called my friend with the private jet, who was always willing to rescue me, and he and his girlfriend offered to come pick me up at the nearest airport. But I had no idea where that was or how to find out. So I ended up getting a ride with this woman from Make-A-Wish who happened to drive by and see me on the side of the road, sobbing and streaked with cake.

When I went to my doctor to get checked out and make sure the baby was okay, I said I had fallen down. It was that same old story of trying to hold everything together. And I was always real good at making excuses for John in my mind. So by the time I had cooled down and found out that he hadn't hurt the baby, I was telling myself that he was just so drunk he hadn't known what he was doing. The alternatives were too hard to face. And, at the very least, I had gotten in a few good licks against those nasty-ass strippers. I'll always be proud of that.

And, of course, John was sorrier than ever. When he did something so terrible, as I was about to learn again and again, he was always equally apologetic. As soon as he got back to the Arkansas house, he found me and tried to make it right.

"I'm so sorry," he said. "I'm so sorry. I want you to go on a trip. I'll pay. Just call Angela, and you all can go to Destin or whatever."

"Really?" I said.

Right about then, I was pretty happy about the idea of getting away from him for a few days. Plus, when he had behaved that badly, I did feel like it was my due to enjoy as much shopping and good living as I could. But I was hesitant too. First of all, I was a little surprised that he'd suggested it, no matter how bad he felt.

John hated to be alone, and he was terribly jealous. By that point, I barely even went out to dinner with my friends, even though that was one of my favorite things to do, just because he always threw such a fit. It wasn't worth it. So for him to offer this trip was a big deal.

"Well what are *you* going to do?" I asked.

"I'm just going to go to Houston by myself," he said.

John loved to take off on road trips in his bus, even when he didn't have to be anywhere for a tournament or an outing, so this didn't surprise me. I went to Florida with my friend Angela, and we had fun. I almost felt like I had to, because it seemed so important to John that I did. Not that I needed to try that hard where shopping and eating were concerned.

John seemed sorry, but even if he was, that didn't stop him from doing exactly what he wanted to do. Only this was the year when he couldn't seem to get away with his lies anymore. I got a call from one of my friends in Houston, and she told me that a woman with reddish-brown hair had been seen getting off John's bus the night before. I didn't like the sound of that because Houston was where Shanae lived, and so I called John. He acted like it was no big deal.

"Who was the girl that got off the bus at two o'clock in the morning?" I said.

"That was the security guy's wife," he said. "That wasn't Shanae."

Of course it *was* Shanae. Only I didn't find out until years later. At the time, I didn't have any proof, and I was still wanting to believe him, so I let it go. I mean, who would want to think that her husband was making up for basically abusing his *preg-*

nant wife by sending her on a trip so he could go hook up with his ex-girlfriend?

Even though I didn't believe him for one minute that it was the security guard's wife, I told myself that there was probably some good explanation and left it at that. I was busy getting ready for Little John's arrival, and it was easy to block out the bad stuff and just focus on the good. And I forgave him for the cake incident because that's what I did. I was always, always, always forgiving him.

The rest of the time, what he did more of was to leave the house and not come home for three days, which was bad enough. And then he started this new thing where, not only would he leave me at home alone, without any warning and sometimes without any money, but he would change his cell phone number too, so I couldn't track him down, even if I needed something. One time I had to borrow $100 from a friend to get gas. And this was when we had a lot of money. But while he could be very generous with me, and I was very aware of how lucky I was that I got to spend as much money as I did on the house and the kids, and drive the nice cars that I did, and wear the expensive jewelry, he always controlled how much money I had. And he always kept me in a financial situation where I needed him, especially when he was unhappy with me, and even more so when he had done something and he was scared that I might leave him. During those times, he never gave me money until he knew the little bit he had given me was gone, so I couldn't have left, even if I'd decided I needed to get away.

Well, I shouldn't have wanted to be going anywhere that summer. And John shouldn't have either. Our beautiful son, Little John Daly, whom we had both wanted so much, was born on July 23.

But we didn't have much chance to enjoy his arrival. Just over a week later, on Austin's birthday on August 4, I found out that I was being indicted in the money-laundering case that my dad had gotten caught up in.

Now, when I got the call, John was up at our house in Arkansas, even though I'd just delivered his first son, and because of the size I am and the fact that Little John was almost nine pounds when he delivered, they'd had to give me stitches from ass to elbow afterward. And I was so upset and scared that I might be taken away from my babies and put in jail, that all I wanted was to be with John and feel like everything was going to be okay. I was in Oxford, Mississippi, at the time, and I wasn't even supposed to be driving, but I did it anyhow. It took me about five hours, and I was in agony the whole time. I was anxious and scared about the indictment and trying not to let the kids see. Plus I was in physical pain because it put so much pressure on my stitches for me to sit for that length of time. I was dying and taking pain medicine, and just focusing on getting to John. I finally got home and right into bed. I was still hurting, but at least John was being sweet.

"I love you," he kept saying. "I love you."

And all this other stuff about how it was going to be okay and we were going to get through this together. Finally, he went into the other room. And my phone rang. It was my mom, calling to say that she had some mail or something for John, and she wanted to know what he wanted her to do with it. I told her that he was smoking outside on the porch. I got up and hobbled out there to ask him about it.

Only he was gone. He had gotten on his bus, without saying a single word to me, and driven off. I should have known that all of those loving things he had been saying weren't worth anything. He'd been up there in Arkansas with all of his troll friends, and I'm sure his agent and his ex-wives had been calling him too, and everyone was telling him that he should leave me because of the indictment. Never mind that we had a baby at home who was less than two weeks old.

So there I was, alone with the baby. Austin, who was four at the time, was the only other person who was there with me. Because of my stitches, I couldn't even lift the baby, so Austin had to help me put Little John to bed and change him. Not that I had anything to change the baby into because we'd loaded all of the baby stuff onto the bus in advance of a trip we were about to leave on, so John had not only driven off and left me. He'd also taken all of the baby clothes and supplies with him.

On top of all of the stress, I was scared. That house in Arkansas was very secluded. And the only people in the area that I was really close with at that point were my brother and sister-in-law, and she was out of town. So I tried to call John, figuring I could reason with him. But no, he had changed his phone number.

The time that followed immediately after this, I don't remember so well. I'm pretty certain that I had a nervous breakdown. I was a wreck, and then for John to disappear like that just made it all the worse. I was crying uncontrollably, day and night. I was in pain. I was trying to take care of a small child and a newborn by myself. I had no idea what to do. I couldn't drive myself home to Memphis. I was telling my parents not to come get me.

Even when I'm at my lowest, I've always taken care of myself. And I wouldn't be done like that. Luckily, I'm the best investigator there is. So I called the phone company, acting like I was lost in the woods or some equally dramatic story that made it seem like I absolutely needed to get in touch with John, and we'd just gotten a new phone number and, silly me, I hadn't written it down good enough. So they gave me his new number. I knew his password because I had set up his voice mail account for him, and so I checked his messages. Well that was an eye-opener.

Apparently he had left me.

There was a voice mail from his ex-wifey number two, saying that she and his ex-wifey number three were so glad that he had gotten rid of me because he could do so much better. I didn't even know what to think at first. I mean, to be that cruel, and then to be such a coward about it too.

Through the messages, I came to realize that John had gone to Texas to hook up with his ex-fiancée, Shanae. That put me over the edge. If I had been a mess before, I was a total disaster now. But I'd been lucky enough to get to know, through my friend Alex, two of the best people in the world, Sean and Kim Snipes, during the early years of my marriage. And Kim had me come right over to her house so she could load me up with all of these hand-me-down baby clothes that had belonged to her kids. We started drinking some wine. And we were just laughing and laughing—which was something I needed to do very badly at the time—because we'd decided it would be fun to iron clothes for some reason. And Kim didn't know how to iron, so I was showing her how. We got to talking about what I should do about John, and like before, I really just wanted to make him stand up and be a man about what he was doing to our family. She offered to buy me a plane ticket, since I didn't have any money of my own, and watch Austin for me while I tracked down John and confronted him. As we were making my travel plans, I finally started to feel things turn around and I found myself thinking: *I'm fine, we can do this, but he's going to tell me to my face. We're going to talk about this.*

John had gone to Texas to do an outing for his sponsors at 84 Lumber, and from there he went to New York in their private plane. As usual, the people at 84 Lumber were so good to my family and me. John might not like this very much, but they told me exactly where he would be and when. And so, even though I wasn't really supposed to fly with a baby that young, I took Little John and went to find John and have it out with him once and for all.

I pulled up to where the bus was parked in a Chevy Suburban, all blacked out, and I got straight out of the car and carried Little John up to the bus. At first, Donnie and the other trolls wouldn't let me on, but I knew the code to unlock the door and finally managed to get past them. Now, John'd been gone for three or four days, during which time he'd changed his phone number, so I hadn't talked to him about where he'd been or what he'd been up to, and I was busy putting the clues together. Inside, of course, there was a girl's pink razor in the bathroom. And my Louis Vuitton purse was gone.

When I got to the back of the bus, I found John sitting in the bedroom. I can't quite describe what it was, but—aside from the obvious betrayal—it just felt like there was something wrong. John was like this weirdo-looking person that I didn't even know anymore. It wasn't like he looked a particular way; he just didn't seem like my John. He was watching the Playboy channel.

"You're so gross," I said, too shocked to be really angry.

"Sherrie," he said. "Listen to me." Like there was anything he could have said right then that I would have wanted to hear.

"You know what?" I said. "My plane's leaving soon. I came here because, if you want to get a divorce, here's my face, here's your son. All you need to do is tell me that that's what you want to do, and you've got it."

Of course, he didn't like the sound of that. He could run off and do whatever he wanted for however long he wanted, but I was supposed to believe that he really cared about me and about keeping our family together, and I was supposed to be right there waiting for him whenever he decided he wanted to come home to us.

"Don't leave," he said. "I'm sorry. After you got indicted, everybody was telling me that you were a drug dealer, and that I should leave you."

Well, that I believed at least. I'm sure that everyone in his life—his agent, his ex-wives, and the trolls—were telling him that he should get rid of me.

And you know what? I got it. I might have freaked out too if somebody wrote all of those things in the paper about him, and if all of my friends were filling my head full of negative thoughts— which, surprisingly, given how badly John behaved, they never did. I could see how he might have really thought that I was nothing but trouble. So I kind of let him slide on that part at least. The fact that he had left me with a newborn baby and no money, that was another matter altogether. But he seemed to feel really awful about that and to dote on Little John when he saw him.

"I'm so sorry for doing that to you," he said.

And, although it probably should have taken a lot more than that, I forgave him.

He was particularly good for a while after that, and so I

believed him. For once, he wasn't saying one thing and doing another. He was actually very supportive, which meant so much to me, especially after everything we'd been through and because I was still having all of my legal troubles. When John was good, he was really good. And he was a great dad. I like to sleep late, so he would do the morning shift. He would get up with Little John. He would change diapers. And he was very attentive to Austin. Every day, he took him out to breakfast, and then he'd do things with him, like hit golf balls out behind the house. But best of all, he finally did something that I'd been wanting him to do since we'd gotten married. Of course, he did it in typical John Daly fashion, but I wouldn't have expected anything less from him by then.

We had just been at the PGA Championship the week before. From there, we traveled to Lake Tahoe for a golf tournament, where we met up with Mark and Mary Ellen and a bunch of the guys who worked for their car dealership. This was a day when, for once, we were all partying and having fun without any drama or broken glass. My good friend Alex was flying out to meet us, and she'd told me that I'd better have a bottle of Cristal waiting for her when her flight got in, and that's exactly what I did.

This is actually the worst thing I've ever done as a mother, but I said I was going to tell on myself, so here it is. And, looking back at least, it's kind of a funny story. I wasn't drinking the whole bottle of Cristal, but I did have a glass in the car, and okay, so I probably shouldn't have been drinking and driving at all, but I was.

When I picked up Alex at the airport, I thought I was being funny, and I popped the cork on the bottle of Cristal just as Alex got into the car. Well, it hit the roof so hard that it flew into the back, where Little John was strapped into his baby seat. He started crying, and I was afraid to turn around and look to see what had happened to him.

"Oh my God, what if I just put my baby's eye out with a cork in the car?" I said. "What if I killed him or something?"

He was okay. I think he was crying because he was scared from the noise. But he had two eyes at least. That's all I was concerned about.

So it was that kind of day, and it got more and more fun from there. Well, the next thing we knew, there was a rain delay. John only had one hole left to play, and no one would have ever thought that they would decide to call him back for just one hole. So we were all at the casino, where we were staying, and the rooms were fabulous. We had our doors open, so people were stopping by, and we were having the best time. John wasn't drinking that much that day, at least not for him, so I could actually relax and enjoy myself too. In fact, it was the women who were drinking a lot. I think we drank five bottles of champagne that day. A couple of the players' wives were present, and Billy Mayfair and his wife, Tammy, came by and joined in the festivities for a minute. She was such a kick. I loved her, and I was sad that they ended up getting a divorce too.

Well, all of a sudden, Donnie came sulking on in. Excuse my language, but he was always such a little turd. He was like this little bitty guy who would rain on anything good that was happening. He and I had never gotten along, but after several years of tension, it was finally coming to a head. It reached a point where everything he did made me so incredibly annoyed. He had this crazy way of looking at people, and finally I couldn't take it anymore. I was done being nice.

"Why are you looking at me all crazy?" I said when I saw him.

I'd had words with John about him too. Now, I knew they were friends since the first grade and all of that, but John was still paying him a ridiculous amount to drive the bus, even after I'd said something to him about it. Even more insane, Donnie had actually told John around that time that he thought he should be earning much more. I wasn't there to see it, but John told me how it had gone down.

"I should be making as much as your ex-wives," Donnie said. "I mean, I've been with you longer than them."

"Can you believe he said that?" John asked me afterward. "He thinks he should get what my kids and my ex-wives get. Is he crazy?"

So tensions were already simmering. And Donnie didn't help matters at all by coming into the party with his usual sour expression on his face.

"They just called John back to play," Donnie said.

By then John was taking a nap, passed out on the couch in our room.

"This is great," Donnie said sarcastically.

Well, I can't blame John for this one, since I was a part of causing his screwup on this particular day, instead of just being among the wreckage he left in his crazy, drunken wake. But at least I decided to take charge of the situation.

"Donnie, I'm going to make the executive decision here," I said. "You need to call them and tell them that John is sick. He has a virus, and he is throwing up. He is not going to be able to make it back out on the course today."

"What?" Donnie said, getting even more ticked off at taking orders from me.

"That's what's got to happen," I said. "Go make this work, Donnie."

Well, he was just disgusted by us, and he stormed on out of there. It was for the best, though, because there was no way John would have been able to play, even though it certainly would not have been his first, or his last, drunk game of golf.

So the next day, the men were all at the bar, and Donnie came up between John and his sponsors and interrupted their conversation.

"I'm telling you right now, if you don't leave her, I'm quitting," he said.

John looked at him like he was nuts.

"Bye," John said. "It was good to know you."

Donnie stood there like he couldn't believe it. But John meant it, all right.

And then John whipped it out and peed on the floor right there at the bar. John was always pissing on stuff, and normally it made me crazy. This was the only time I didn't get mad at him, though. I thought it was appropriate, like he was showing Donnie exactly what we thought of him. Not that I was thrilled that he publicly pissed on the floor, of course, because now there was a huge wet spot in this really nice room at the hotel. But since he was kind of doing it for my benefit, I let it slide. See, John did have a romantic side. He just showed it in his own special way.

And so Donnie got on a flight that day and left us there. And he never came back. I couldn't have been happier about that. There was just one problem: He was the bus driver, and John had to be at an 84 Lumber event in Pennsylvania, *immediately*. We had a new caddie, because John's longtime caddie had just quit the week before, and we had to make the caddie drive. He had never driven a bus before, but there was no other way we were going to make it in time. John and the caddie took turns and drove the whole way straight through, because Donnie had left us high and dry. That's exactly the kind of friend he was. At least that one time, I could be happy that John stood up for me.

five

THE SECRET OF
THE SIXTEENTH HOLE

ONNIE'S EXIT was the one bright spot in what was otherwise a pretty bad year. Luckily, by then, I'd made friends with a few of the other players' wives. Once their stories of what it meant to be a player's wife came out, I was at least relieved to discover I wasn't alone. My friend Nicole Kuehne was suspicious that her husband, Hank, was cheating with a woman who worked at the clubhouse at Southwind, where John and I lived. Nicole sent me and a friend of mine who's a lawyer to do a little investigating. Hank had gone to Las Vegas to work with this big golf coach based out there, and

Nicole had a feeling he had the girl with him. We went down to the clubhouse and started talking to people she worked with, only to find she wasn't at work that day because she was away. In Las Vegas. Hank and Nicole ended up getting a divorce. But this girl wasn't done with the golf world. Once she broke up their marriage, she moved on and married another golfer.

Sometimes the players just wanted sex. There was a girl we'd been hearing about for years in relation to what I'll call the Secret of the Sixteenth Hole. I'd been told by many men in Memphis, including my banker, that there was a girl who'd give golfers blow jobs when they got to the sixteenth hole at Southwind. They didn't set it up in advance or anything. Apparently, all they had to do was show that they were ready to pay $300 when they got there, and she'd take them into the bushes and do it for them right there.

There were plenty of professional hookers around at certain spots on Tour too. If the tournament at Dallas was known for all of the strippers that come out, I would have to say that Myrtle Beach is known for prostitutes. Or at least I heard that John had a couple staying with him one year when he was down there to play. Another time, I was with John at a tournament in North Carolina and we literally had to run some prostitutes off. We were walking out to the car in the special parking lot reserved for PGA players, and they came right up to us, even though I was clearly with John.

"Get away from the car," John said to the girls.

I was shocked and totally fascinated. I turned around to look out the window at them as we drove away. I'd never seen real prostitutes before. Or if I had, I hadn't known what they were.

"Were those really prostitutes?" I asked.

"Yeah," John said, laughing because I looked so shocked.

Well, of course I was. They were out there, soliciting in these big rubber heels. They looked like they were straight off the street, like how they looked in *Pretty Woman*. Not Julia Roberts, but the bad ones in *Pretty Woman*.

From what I saw over the years, I think a lot of the players had girls on the side, whether for just one night or an actual affair. There was a well-known story about the time Greg Norman's wife, Laura, took the rest of the players' wives over to see the new yacht she and Greg had bought, only to find him on board with some little honey of his. Not long after that, Laura says, tennis player Chris Evert broke up her three-decade marriage by pursuing Greg right in front of her. And everyone had heard about another top PGA Tour player who had to pay a stripper a million dollars because he got her pregnant while he was married. But none of the wives gossiped about each other or talked much about any of the bad behavior. There wasn't a lot of personal business being spread around. I've seen that other women can be catty and talk trash, but I don't remember any of the wives ever not liking each other or being mean to each other. I think they understood they were all in it together, and if anyone's husband did cut up, the other women were sympathetic because they knew their husband could easily be next. In fact, all of us came to realize that when we got pregnant, and we couldn't go out on Tour as much anymore, that was the kiss of death for our marriages because that's when the cheating always started. And then, when we did come out on Tour, we'd be walking the course, watching our husbands play, trying to act like everything was good and we were happy, even when we weren't.

Now, in my *close circle* of friends, we all knew each other's dirt and we'd do spy trips for each other. Actually, come to think of it, I really didn't have to spy on anyone's husband. Most of *their husbands* were doing what they were supposed to be doing. My friends were usually spying for me.

There was one area where the wives could be a little catty; that had to do with how much money their husbands let them spend. All of the wives went to Louis Vuitton. Everyone was always getting a new handbag. The diamonds just kept getting bigger and bigger. Mine included. All of the ladies on the PGA Tour started getting the same ring, which had a big square diamond with a smaller square diamond on each side. Well, I wanted my wedding ring to look different, and I found this picture of a queen's ring in an encyclopedia of old antique jewelry. I had a jeweler make a replica. It was this gorgeous dome ring that looked like an estate piece, and it was huge: 14.9 karats in all. It wasn't just me who cared about jewelry, though. John's feelings got hurt if I didn't display the pieces he gave me. I always wore a Rolex masterpiece or a Harry Winston or Franck Muller watch too. During those years, whenever I looked at what J. Lo had on in the magazines, I'd think: *Oh, I have that.*

A lot of us players' wives loved to shop. We spent much of our free time together working the credit cards. When the PGA organized wives' days out on Wednesdays, it was often a trip to a mall. Or sometimes we'd go to a spa, which was really nice too. When we were in New Orleans, we stayed at the Ritz, and Emeril cooked lunch for us.

For me, shopping was always the most fun, and retail therapy was one of my best means for getting through the dark days with John. In the beginning, when I found out the first bad things he did, I'd cry and yell and carry on. After a few years, and the fact that the things he did kept getting worse and worse, I hit my limit and stopped crying. Instead, when I got upset, I'd go online and buy expensive things that could hopefully make my life beautiful. My friend Amy Campbell, who's married to Chad Campbell, told me a story that explains it best. She went on this shopping bender one time after she and Chad had an argument, and all of her girlfriends noticed just how much she was spending.

"Amy, why are you buying all of this expensive stuff?" we said.

"Because these things make me feel the way he doesn't: special," she said.

"That is the best line ever," I said.

Of course, we all come up with excuses to turn things around when we spend too much. And Amy and Chad are actually making it work. But her words could have just as easily applied to my marriage to John, even though I didn't realize it at the time. My life might have sucked, but I wanted everything to be beautiful around me. Like if I got a new car or found just the right rug for the living room, it might make me happy. I realized, years later, that you wake up one day and you don't care about any of the stuff you've bought. And it finally dawned on me how miserable I was, but back then, I was still a long way from that. Over the years, it was almost like I worked out a payment system, or maybe I should call it a payback system. Every time John got caught with another phone call from some piece of trash he'd slept with, or another girlfriend he'd gotten back together with, it cost him thirty grand. I know that's a lot of money, but I was generous with it too. I'd buy new outfits for my friends and my mother, take us all out to lunch. And it actually worked out well for me later that I once bought as much as I did. When John left me with nothing at the end of our marriage, and I was broke and I had no money to pay the bills, let alone buy new things, my kids and I still had plenty of clothes. We still looked nice. So at least I could always fake it pretty good. In the beginning, I used the money I had to buy stuff to fake the happiness I wanted; and in the end, I used the stuff I'd bought when I was unhappy to fake the money I no longer had.

I may have been unhappy, but the shopping itself was fun. I can still remember my first $30,000 day. I was in Boston traveling with John and the PGA Tour. My friend Mary Ellen was in town too. I was upset about something John had done, probably having to do with his ex-wifey number three or one of the other women. And so Mary Ellen and I went out to try to cheer me up, and we started drinking vodka martinis. We went to this cute pizza place and ate this whole large thin-crust pizza with this amazing hot, spicy oil that we were pouring all over it. That was one of the best meals I've ever had. Every time the waitress came over, we weren't quite ready to leave yet.

"Oh, we'll have one more round."

"We'll have one more."

After we drank all of these martinis, we decided to go to the mall. We just glided right into Gucci and started picking up all of these beautiful purses. Well, Mary Ellen had never bought a designer bag. At least not until I corrupted her.

"Mary Ellen," I said. "Your husband gambles, your husband drinks. You don't ever buy anything for yourself. If you want it, get it. He won't care."

After she bought the first one, she was out of control. So she was like, well, if we get the big purse, we might as well get the little purse and the shoes to go with it. So we ended up with red shoes, green shoes, brown shoes, black shoes, little purse, big purse. I don't even know everything that we bought by the end of that spree. I know that my purchases alone totaled thirty thousand dollars.

Later that month, the bill came in.

"I can't believe you did that," John said when he saw it. But he couldn't get really mad or take away my credit card because he had done something bad that he was trying to make up to me. That's how it always was between us, and I ended up spending a lot of money over the years.

One of the biggest shopping days of my life was with my friend Amy Campbell, who had the great line about why all of us players' wives spent as much as we did. I don't know what got into me. I wasn't even mad about anything, but we sure lived it up. John and Amy's husband, Chad, were doing an outing together in Delaware. I'm sure they were getting paid a nice penny, probably $50,000 or $100,000 each. We had a limo for the day, and of course we didn't want to go out with them to watch them play boring golf. The wives always seemed to make their way to the mall. Not only was it our therapy, but it was a perk to traveling all of the time and not having any life other than that. Amy and I were pleasantly surprised to discover that there's this fantastic mall in Delaware. It had Versace, Gucci, everything two players' wives with a Louis Vuitton wallet full of credit cards could ever want. Amy and I got a bottle of vodka and made these two big-gulp drinks. We had the limo take us to the mall, and the retail marathon began. We were having the day of our life, just shopping and shopping without pause. We went to Versace. We went to Chanel; that was the first time I ever bought a $5,500 bag. It was hot pink, of all colors. By the time we were done, we had bags and bags of stuff. And John and Chad were both calling us, telling us that our private planes were due to leave.

"Y'all are late," John said the first time he called.

But we were trying to finish up in this one store.

They kept calling back, and by now they were bitching.

"Where are y'all?" John said. "We've got to go."

Finally we were done, and we managed to get all of our fabulous new items into the limo. But we knew that we were in trouble. So we gave the limo driver $100 to get on the phone and lie for us and say that he had gotten lost or been in a traffic jam, so it wouldn't be our fault. But when we finally got to the airport, they knew exactly what we had been doing. And the bags kind of gave us away too.

Chad and Amy were on one private plane and John and I were on another. We didn't have the kids that day, but we still had his caddie and his clubs and all of our luggage. There was not a lot of room for extra stuff. And I had a lot of extra stuff.

"Oh my God, what is all of this?" John said. "You know we don't have any room. Why didn't you ship this?"

"I just bought a few things," I said.

And then I looked more closely at the bags.

"This isn't mine," I said.

Well, I guess Chad was bitching on Amy, so she had told him that none of the bags were hers and had put them all over by my plane. Now, I had done a lot of shopping that day, but it looked like I had done an *insane* amount of shopping. I took the rap for both of us, and we barely got it all home. We were all squished on there with all of these bags. I took a few cussings over that. Our bank was set up so that when I went over a certain amount, the money dipped down in his account, and so he really noticed it. I think that was the third big bender I had been on, so he took away my card.

"That's it," he said.

And it wasn't even all my fault. I called Amy when I got home.

"I can't believe you did that to me," I said.

"Just ship it to me," she said, laughing. "I wasn't going down like that."

I met one of my best friends right around then, and because she was also married to a professional athlete, she had a much better idea of what I was going through with John than almost anyone else did. John and I were back in Memphis between tournaments, and we went to a charity event downtown at the Gibson Guitar Factory. He told me that his friends Mike Miller and Jason Williams from the Memphis Grizzlies were going to be there with their wives, Jennifer Miller and Danika Williams. Well, Jennifer and I just hit it off immediately. Danika was real sweet too, but Jason got traded soon after that, so I never got to know her that well.

Jennifer and I, though, we were like sisters or something right away. The guys went off to do their thing, so I was just standing there, a little nervous and awkward because I was around all these new people. But without any effort, Jennifer and I automatically started talking and talking. She had just had a baby, and Little John wasn't very old, so we had that in common. And we were both a wreck: me because I'd just caught John cheating, and Jennifer because she was still losing her baby weight, and she'd just ruined her car, and there was all this drama in her life too. So we were commiserating about all of this bad stuff, and she decided we needed to do a Jägerbomb. Well, I'd never had one before. But, clearly, I like to drink, so I was up for trying something new from behind the bar. She showed me how to drop the shot of Jäger and drink it real fast, and of course I loved it and decided we had to do another. And we've been close friends ever since.

Well, soon after that, John and Mike were playing golf together. So Jennifer and I went to meet them at the course. And I don't know what it was about that day in particular, but I broke down and started crying in her car.

"John's been cheating," I said.

I was boo-hooing away, and then she started crying along with me.

I knew what would make me feel better, but I was afraid to use my cell phone to do it, because I had just been indicted, and I was worried that the feds might be listening to my calls. But she was so sweet that I figured she might help me.

"Can I borrow your cell phone?" I asked her.

She handed it over, no questions asked. I called Shanae right up.

"Let me tell you something, Shanae," I said. "If you do not leave my husband alone, and quit calling my house, I'm going to tie bricks on your feet, and you're going to be swimming with the fish on the bottom of the river. Leave me the fuck alone."

Jennifer and I were just like dying out laughing.

Of course, Shanae had to go and call Judge Biggers in Oxford, Mississippi, who was handling my case and who already had it out for me. Well, Shanae ratted me out and said I'd threatened her. Of course I denied it and said she was lying. Shanae said she had a recording of the call, but they never could prove it was me because it wasn't made from my cell phone.

Now that's what friends are for. Anyone else might have

thought I was crazy for talking to Shanae like that, but Jennifer lived in the same world, so she understood how hard it was to be a wife in the PGA or the NBA or whatever professional sport it was. Our husbands were gone so much that we were basically single moms, and we didn't have anyone to help us with our kids. Yes, we were incredibly lucky because we could afford to have someone help us. But that's another reason Jennifer and I got along so well. Neither of us felt right having a nanny. I didn't want a nanny changing my kids' diapers. I think it creates a bond to do that for your child.

Everyone always looked at us and thought we were these spoiled bitches who had it made because we had these big houses and fancy cars, and we were able to go shopping and buy ourselves expensive things. And of course, we did have it good. We felt extremely fortunate, especially that our children were so well taken care of, but we also knew in a way that most people couldn't understand: There's a price to be paid for the good life. It can be incredibly lonely.

Not only were our husbands never home, but someone always wanted their time and attention whether they were home or not. Some buddies, or cousins, or friends, or brothers—well, I can't say anything bad about John's brother, because he's always been nothing but nice to me, but *someone* close to them—were always trying to get closer by getting rid of us wives and trying to take our place because they wanted access to the money and the VIP treatment.

And there was always somebody who wanted to hook our husbands up with a model or some hot chick. And even when we got mad or hurt about this, we couldn't let our feelings show, or be even the littlest bit of a bitch, because there was always somebody else waiting to take our spot. And no matter what they did, we couldn't even punish our husbands because they could just leave us and have whomever else they wanted. Really and truly, it was hard not to be miserable sometimes and to feel bought.

Of course, let's be honest, the retail therapy did help.

So did being able to afford to buy bottles of Grey Goose and make Jell-O shots at ten in the morning. We'd sit outside, turn the music up, and drink them all day. Sometimes that helped too. Or we'd get a driver, or a friend who didn't drink, so we could go out to eat and have cocktails on Main Street in downtown Memphis, live it up a little, and not have to answer to anyone. I'm just so glad we were in it together. Of course, the best part of all of this is that Mike and Jennifer actually made it and are happier than ever.

But in some ways, Jennifer had it worse than me because the NBA wives don't really travel with their husbands, so she got left at home a lot more than I did. Of course, with some of the times that John and I had on the road, maybe being with him wasn't really so enviable. That September, John and I got back on the bus and traveled to the Bell Canadian Open. While we were there, John's little spell as a loving, devoted husband came to an end. We were staying on the bus in this parking lot near the tournament, and I woke up one night, and he was sitting up by himself, watching—what else?—the Playboy channel. It just grossed me out so much, seeing my husband looking at these skanks when I was right there in bed, and I got so mad at him.

"What are you up watching dirty TV for and being all sneaky about it?" I said.

Of course, he didn't have any good excuse. And I lost my

temper, which is definitely my fault, not his. Anyway, I took an ashtray, and I threw it at the TV and broke the screen right out.

So he got really angry at me then. And his reaction, as usual, was to decide that he was going to leave me in this parking lot by myself. He ran off the bus into the courtesy car and was about to drive away. Well, he wasn't going to leave me in some foreign country all by myself in the bus, with no way to get myself any-where. So I tore off after him, and, well, this is a little embarrass-ing, but this is another spot where I've got to tell on myself. The truth is that I always sleep naked, and because I had just woken up, and I was in such a state about not getting left there by myself, I ran off that bus and out into the parking lot without any clothes on. It's not like there was anyone around to see me, but I guess that's kind of a wild thing to do. I certainly would never do any-thing like that if I had a second to think about it. But I didn't. I was running on adrenaline.

I climbed into the car after him, and in order to stop him, I grabbed his big tacky gold lion-head necklace that he always wore. Well, it broke off in my hand, but at least that slowed him down, and I was able to grab the keys away from him. Once I had them, I ran back onto the bus and locked the door behind me. So now *he* was the one who was stuck out in the parking lot with no means of getting himself out of there.

He was all worked up, and he called a friend of his to come get him. They tried to say later that I was attempting to kill him, which of course wasn't true. And they said that he was so upset and banged up by what I did to him that he missed the cut that day. The reality is that he had already missed the cut, and it had nothing to do with me. He played badly because he'd been out drinking the night before. Actually, he had been drinking heavy the whole time we were there, so he was a total mess. In fact, it was during that trip that he did something that probably humiliated me more than almost anything else he did during our entire marriage—and obviously that's no small feat, what with all the drinking, gambling, and whoring around. Like most things with John, he kept it hidden for as long as he could. So I didn't find out what he had been up to until a few months later. But that night on the bus, I knew he had been out somewhere.

Of course, he acted like he was so innocent. He even called my dad and told on me, like we were kids or something. My dad is real old fashioned, so he was not at all happy to have to ask me if I'd been outside of the bus naked. I didn't want to upset him, and I knew there was no way I could explain myself, so I think I actually lied to my dad and said I hadn't done it. I told my mom, though. She knows all.

So right after that, during the last weekend of September, we went to the Valero Texas Open and John just kept on with the craziness. He got disqualified, and he was so mad about missing the cut that he went straight back to the bus and just went nuts. We had bought a new bus that was really nice. It had cost us something like $1.4 million. But it wasn't like he ever put it together that, because we had spent so much money on something, maybe we should take care of it or try to keep it nice. No, he didn't think at all. He just tore it up completely. Not only did he smash out all the windows, which was pretty standard for him. He actually knocked out the windshield that time too, which isn't exactly easy to do.

I remember I was so embarrassed because Rory and Amy Sabbatini had parked their bus right behind us, and her mom and dad, who I just loved, were standing out there watching my husband be the lunatic that only he could be. I walked up and all I heard was this *bang, bang, bang,* as he smashed out the windows one by one. And then he got behind the wheel and raced out of there so fast that the bus was rocking, and I thought it was going to tip over. Now, the craziest part about that day was that he wasn't even drunk. That was what he was like when he was sober too. He couldn't even make any excuses for his behavior. I guess that was the real him.

So we went home to Memphis after that, and even I couldn't deny that we were definitely having problems. In fact, I was so fed up with everything he'd put me through that I was finally getting ready to divorce him. And John told this writer for *Sports Illustrated,* in an article that came out in late October, that he had intended to file for a divorce earlier that same month. So we were kind of in this standoff, where both of us were on the verge of filing the papers, but neither of us had done it yet.

But the weird thing was that, like always happened with us, we'd sometimes have these little moments of calm that were almost like normal married life in the middle of all this craziness. Now, I've always loved Elvis, just absolutely loved him, and growing up in Memphis, I'd been listening to his music and going to Graceland my whole life. Lisa Marie Presley was giving a concert in Memphis, and we got tickets. I was beyond excited to go, because I knew that if I went with John, we'd be able to go backstage and meet her. And for me, that was pretty much the most thrilling thing ever. I mean, we'd met so many celebrities over the years, and we were friends with musicians whose music I'd listened to on the radio, but this was Elvis Presley's own flesh and blood. I was beside myself.

So we had driven back to Memphis from Arkansas that day, and John dropped me off at the house so I could get ready while he went off to do some errands. He was going to come back to pick me up, and then we were going to go to the concert together. So I got all dressed up, and I was in the best mood. Only the time came for him to come get me, and he didn't show up. So I called him. And he didn't answer his phone. Well, that wasn't a good sign. It got later and later, and still there wasn't any sign of him. And I kept calling him and calling him, but I couldn't get through. Well, I'd been through this enough times before to know what was coming. So, no, I never did get to see Lisa Marie Presley. And, yes, John had taken off on me again. But he didn't just go to Texas this time. He went to Korea. That's right, instead of coming home to take me to a concert like we'd planned, he'd gotten on a plane and flown to Korea to play in a golf tournament without saying one single word to me about it.

The next thing I heard, he'd gone from Korea to Las Vegas, without talking to me once this whole time, and he was spotted there with his ex-wifey number three. Now, I was furious when I heard this, but I wasn't exactly surprised either. She'd been all over John ever since my indictment. She was always calling John and telling him that he should leave me. And their daughter, Sierra, told me that she had heard John calling her mom "sweetheart." I still don't know what there was between them while John and I were married, but I could only assume it wasn't good for my relationship with him, given that my husband had just gotten home from an overseas trip and he was in Las Vegas with her, not me.

Remember, when we were first married, John always wanted me around every minute, even when we weren't getting along. He was so jealous, and he couldn't stand to be alone, to the point where he was always saying he was going to kill himself if I ever left him, even just to go to dinner with friends.

So I knew something was up when he didn't ask me to go meet up with him in Vegas. And I was still mad about Lisa Marie too. But he would not answer his phone, so I decided to go to Las Vegas in person and have it out with him. Little John, Austin, and I showed up at the airport in Vegas, just as John got there.

"You're going to talk to me," I said.

He knew he didn't have any choice at this point, so he took me to the hotel so I could check in. Only he got me a room at a different hotel from the one he was staying at. We were married—barely, but we still were. And he didn't want me anywhere near him, not even in a different room at the same hotel. But I came to find out that he didn't have any problem having his ex-wifey number three stay in the room adjoining his suite at the Paris. And I was so mad too, because during this trip he took her to my friend Mary Ellen's house, like he didn't even care about rubbing my face in how little concern he had for my feelings. And he took his ex-wifey out to dinner at Ruth's Chris Steak House, which probably made me even angrier. You see, there's nothing I like more than getting dressed up and going out to eat good food at a nice restaurant. Well, John's idea of a nice restaurant was McDonald's. That man could literally eat at McDonald's three times a day. And if I could ever convince him to eat anything else, there was no way he would ever go to a restaurant with me and have a proper meal where he had to sit across from me and make conversation. No way. Even though we could afford anything we could have wanted, and we could gain access to the most exclusive places everywhere we went, it didn't matter. He made me get everything as takeout. So we traveled all over the world, and I did get to eat meals prepared by some of the best chefs at some of the best restaurants. But it was all eaten out of Styrofoam containers on the bus.

Well, now that I saw how things were—John had his ex-wifey with him at the Paris, while he put the kids and me at Bally's—I decided they could have each other. Once I'd spoken my mind. I went over to the Paris lobby to confront him.

"I'm leaving," I said. "Have her. Do whatever you want."

Well, John caught up with me as I was pushing Little John on out of there in the baby carriage. He tried to get me to stay, but I wasn't about to be stopped.

"I'm leaving," I said. "All I want is a divorce. I don't want anything from you. The prenup can stick. All I want is custody of Little John."

He could tell I was serious about leaving, so he tried to give me some money. He handed me this big wad of bills. Well, I was so mad, I just threw it right back at him. I can still picture those bills flying all over the place in the lobby at the Paris. And, just like that, I turned and walked away, pushing the baby carriage. And I ran right into my good friends Sean and Kim Skipes, who happened to be staying at the Paris just then. I could not have been happier to see two people. They always seemed to come to my rescue.

After that, I called my mom and told her what had happened, and that I needed a plane ticket to get home.

"Do you have any money at all?" she asked.

"Not a cent," I said.

Well, I had meant what I said about the divorce. When I got back to Memphis, I filed divorce papers on October 17, 2003. I had John's brother go and get my stuff for me from the house in Arkansas. But when he pulled up to my parents' house where I was staying, with all of my stuff loaded in his car, the bus was parked in the driveway and John and I were back together. As soon as I finally pushed back on him, he was at my door in an instant. He drove straight from Las Vegas to Memphis. And he made this whole big scene. He said how sorry he was, and how the ex-wifey number three had been saying all of this stuff about the indictment, but that he wouldn't ever listen to her again, and he was just begging me not to leave him. So I figured I had made my point, and I tore up the divorce papers.

Only, as all of this stuff added up over the years, it was getting harder to trust him, with good reason. And when he broke my trust again, like he always seemed to do, it was getting harder for me to forgive him. Sometimes I had to pray it away. I mean, literally, I would just put it in my prayers, day after day: *Don't let me resent him. Get these bad thoughts out of my head. Let me give this a nice chance, so maybe we can be happy again.*

six

WHEN BRETT MICHAELS IS THE VOICE OF REASON, YOU KNOW YOU'RE IN TROUBLE

O F COURSE, once I got my head clear, he always went and did something else. And not just anything, but something big; it always seemed like as soon as I forgave him for one thing, the next stunt he pulled was always a biggie.

He started being especially nice to me, and at first I thought he was making it up to me because of how rotten he had been that fall. But then it was like he was being *too* nice. I had been telling him that I wanted to go to New York City at Christmas with my friends and go shopping in Times Square. And I was kind of waiting on an answer, but I never expected him to let me do it, because he was so possessive and he never wanted me to go anywhere.

All of a sudden, he bought tickets for all of my girlfriends and me to fly to New York and stay for four days, which was so nice of him. But that was the thing: He was being a little *too* nice. I remember I called my friend Angela, and I was talking to her about the whole situation, but we didn't really think too much about it because we were just so happy that we were going to get to have this fabulous trip together.

A little while after we had hung up the phone, she called me back. Now, I've known her since I was fifteen, and I've heard her cry maybe twice in that entire time.

"Sherrie," she said. "I've got to tell you, everybody knows. Everybody in the city knows, everybody in the world knows."

"What are you talking about?" I said.

"John's pictures were on this Web site," she said. "And there's this porn girl. And everybody's sending the pictures around. It's everywhere."

I don't even think I had a computer at the time. So I went to see my good friend Alex, who always traveled with John and me. And together, we prepared for the worst. Finally, I was ready.

"Let me see them," I said.

We didn't have to look very far. The pictures were literally everywhere. They were on ESPN sports and on Golf Channel sports. And they were of John, all right. They had been taken when we were in Canada, and he'd been off at this party, carrying on with this girl who had this porn site called Tiffany.com. There were pictures of both of them lifting their shirts to show off their bare chests to the camera, and a picture of him grabbing her bare breasts, which he had autographed, and another of her grabbing his crotch. And, in all of them, they were just grinning and grinning like they were having the time of their lives.

I felt like he'd just done to me what I'd seen him do to so many windows.

"Oh my God," I said. "Oh my God. Oh my God."

I called John, and there was no hiding how upset I was.

"Well, I guess you heard," he said.

"I'm really not sure," I said. "Maybe I have."

It was like he had done so much bad stuff by that point, I didn't even know what was what anymore, or what exactly he had done. I just knew it was bad, and that here I was, feeling angry and humiliated all over again.

"Well, I'll understand if you divorce me," he said.

"I do not even know what to say," I said. "I don't even know that person in those pictures."

He was quiet on the other end of the line.

"What is wrong with you?" I asked.

He didn't even try to justify himself this time.

"What are you going to do?" he said.

I got really quiet. And when I get really quiet, that's even scarier than when I yell. Because I have no problem speaking my mind, but when I'm beyond that, well, just watch out. And John knew me well enough by then to know that about me, which is probably why he went along with what I said next.

"I guess I'm going to go to New York with my friends and go shopping," I said.

"Anything you want," he said.

He paid for the whole trip. And before I left, he gave me $10,000 in cash. Well, when I had originally asked to go on that trip, I had wanted to go Christmas shopping. And I had thought it would be a good way to cheer up a friend of mine who was all torn up about the way her husband had been such a dog to her. Well, now *I* needed cheering up too. So I didn't go Christmas shopping. When we got to New York, we started partying. I swear I spent the whole $10,000 on Cristal.

The only time I had been to New York as an adult, I had been with John, so of course I'd always had people around to get me into wherever I wanted to go. So I had no idea that we needed to be on the list for clubs or anything like that.

We got all dressed up our first night there, and we got to the first club and waited in line. Finally, we got up to the entrance.

"Are you on the list?" the door guy said.

"No," I said.

But I had $10,000 in cash in my purse, so I didn't think it would be a problem.

"Can we pay to get in?" I said.

Well, this was New York. "You have to be on the list," he said.

They were so cold, not at all like in Memphis, and they shut the door right in our faces. So we got back in the car to regroup.

"Hold on," I said. "I have an idea."

So we went to the next place on my list, which I had made from reading gossip magazines. I knew it was the big club where all the soap opera stars went.

"I'll handle this, ladies," I said. "Let's just walk in."

Security stopped us at the door, of course.

"Are you on the list?" the guy said.

"Yes," I said. "My name is Sherrie, and I need two bottles of Cristal and some strawberry puree."

"Oh, come right this way," he said.

I mean, that cost at least $1,000 right there, so of course they let us in when I said I was going to buy $1,000 worth of booze right up front.

I knew about this special back room they had there because I had read about it in *Star* magazine, so I told them we wanted to go in there. And they let us. We had so much fun that night. I think I spent $2,500 just at that one place. But it was totally worth it. For the first time in months, I was smiling and laughing and not waiting for something awful to happen. Plus I had never had Cristal rosé with strawberry puree in it before. I remember thinking: *This tastes so much better than a new purse.*

We had a ball. We enjoyed the city for four days, and like I said, I spent all that money John gave me. I figured I'd earned it. We stayed at the Waldorf-Astoria, which I knew was where Paris Hilton once lived. And we didn't shop at all. We went to Saks once and we hit up Chinatown. Other than that, all we did was eat and drink, eat and drink. I remember I had the best apple martini of my life on that trip.

John ended up filing a lawsuit against this stripper, Tiffany, who had posted on her Web site all of those pictures of them cavorting like a bunch of drunk, slutty buffoons. Apparently when she had encouraged John to be in the pictures, she had told him that they were just for her and wouldn't be made public (not that this distinction would have made me, THE WIFE, any happier about their existence, but hey, I'm no lawyer). Plus, apparently she said there was going to be some sex video of them, but there wasn't. At least he had some class, right? Actually, who knows? There probably *was* a sex tape and he just paid her off to keep her quiet. Nothing would surprise me. But he did end up winning like $600,000 from that case. I didn't care about the money. Nothing could make those pictures disappear. And nothing could make me stop crying at the fact that they were out there, showing how little respect my husband had for me. Literally, I don't think I stopped crying for a month straight. John finally got so upset that he would have done anything to make it right, or at least get some peace.

"Please tell me, what can I do?" he said. "Anything. Just stop crying."

So he used some of the money from the settlement to buy me a Porsche, which was my dream car. It was beautiful. The only problem was that every time I drove it, I thought of those pictures and that only made me cry harder. We ended up having to sell it because the connection was too strong. See, money really doesn't fix everything.

Things were mostly okay for a while after that, though. When John was in trouble, he definitely tried to make up for it. And I can't be bought, but I had no problem with letting him show me just how sorry he was.

John *was* sorry. And he had good reason to be. But he wasn't the only person I was fed up with. I sure hadn't forgotten that stunt he pulled in Las Vegas. In January 2004, we were in Palm Springs, and that's where ex-wifey number three lives. It didn't help matters at all that she kept calling John, and she came out to the course while he was playing. I understood that she had their daughter, Sierra, with her, and of course I wanted Sierra to be able to see her dad while he was in town. But I didn't understand why ex-wifey had to be wearing these big high heels—and mind you, we were on a golf course. And I think it's already been well established that high heels and manicured greens don't go together (unless you're one of those strippers in the rubber heels down in Dallas). So I watched the ex-wifey strut around all day, and I didn't say anything. And then, finally, I lost it. I must have looked like this little feisty dog, tearing her up out on the golf course.

"I am so sick of seeing your fucking face everywhere I go," I said. "You didn't watch him play when you were married. Why are you watching him now? Just leave me alone."

Of course, she didn't take my warning. Well, that was not a good idea.

John was playing in Palm Springs at an event with Freddy Couples and Roger Clemens. Of course, ex-wifey was following Roger Clemens around too. So all of us were standing there, and I had to speak my mind, as I do.

"Roger, I'm telling you," I said. "Leave this bitch alone. She's going to fuck you up. I'm telling you. Stay away from her. She's evil. She's a home wrecker."

I wasn't crazy to say all of that, either. It just came out in the paper, all of these years later, that she was one of the girlfriends that Roger Clemens was running around with while he was married. Knowing her, she probably called in and reported the story herself because she hoped it would make her famous.

John may have been trying with me around that time, but there was still no telling how he would behave, especially because he was still drinking so heavy, and so I never knew what to expect when we were at a tournament or an outing. But I could usually expect to be embarrassed in some way. Like that spring, when he played the 84 Lumber Classic. Not only were they always John's best sponsor, but this was a PGA event too. I mean, they had all of the big names at their tournament. Of course, John was partying and drinking heavy. That wasn't anything new for him. But this time, he couldn't hold it together. When he went out to play, he literally passed out right there on the golf course. They had to carry him off.

I felt so bad about the whole situation because the people from 84 Lumber had tried to talk to him about his drinking, but there was just no way he'd listen to anyone. As usual, his agent and the people at the PGA covered up for him. They put out this story that he had been the victim of heat exhaustion. More like it was dehydration because he had been so drunk, drinking for days and days, partying almost up until his tee time. Of course he passed out. I'm surprised nothing worse than that happened to him.

John didn't party like a rock star: He partied *harder* than the rock stars. That March, we were in Florida for the VH1 annual "Fairway to Heaven" Celebrity Golf Tournament, and we spent the day hanging out on the bus with Brett Michaels and Tommy Lee, who was dating Mayte Garcia. She was one of the most beautiful women I've ever seen, with this amazing dancer's body. I remember she made me feel better about my own life, because I overheard her on her cell phone, talking about how she'd been spying on Tommy and she was mad about some contact he'd had with Pamela Anderson. I was thinking: *I am not alone. We all have the same struggle.*

Not that I could see what Mayte had to complain about. I fell in love with Tommy. He was so kind. And calm. It was one of those occasions when I could tell that everyone felt bad for me because John was being so loud and rude. I wasn't drinking at all, and I ended up having to be his mom and trying to talk sense into John. Like that was going to happen.

John had always been proud of having an especially large penis, which I guess is why he was always taking it out and peeing on stuff, and so he decided to challenge Tommy to see who was bigger. They both whipped it out right there on the bus. I didn't see, but I did hear that John was bigger around. I'm sure he just loved that.

Finally, it was time for us to leave because we needed to be somewhere else. Austin and I were riding in the back of the bus, and we also had Brett Michaels and some other folks riding up front with us. Well, John started reversing the bus, and he was so drunk that he almost ran something over. I was about to have a fit. I ran to the driver's seat and tried to stop him.

"I'm not riding with you," I said. "We need to stay here. Don't drive."

Of course, John intended to drive, so he didn't stop.

Brett Michaels overheard this and joined us.

"John, you can't drive," Brett said.

Finally John agreed that Brett's personal driver could take over for him. I'll just say this: *When Brett Michaels is the voice of reason, you know you're in trouble.*

John had such a reputation by that point that even President George W. Bush had something to say about John's drinking when we met him that year. We were in Washington, D.C., for John to play the Kemper Open, when we found out that we'd been invited to the White House. I remember John was teasing me that they weren't going to let me in because I'd been indicted. "You're probably the first criminal in the White House," he said. Somehow, I don't quite think so, and yes, they let me in.

Our audience with President Bush was short because his arrival had been delayed, but I was definitely impressed by him during the little time we spent with him. He was so charming and nice, and funny too. When he came in, he went right up to John and said, "So, are you still off the sauce?"

Of course we all laughed politely, but it had been a long time since John had been anything close to sober.

Largely because of John's drinking, that was a horrible time for John and me. But I did have the chance to do something that fall that I was really proud of. The PGA did a lot of wonderful charity work, and they gave the players' wives many opportunities to volunteer for different events and fundraisers. I tried to help in any way that I could, but because John and I were always on the road with the kids, I didn't really get the chance to do as much of the hands-on helping as I would have liked.

Now, I was always really proud of all of the events John participated in to raise money for Make-A-Wish and the Boys and Girls Clubs (even if so many of them were disasters for us personally). But I felt like a lot of charities weren't run as well as they could be, with the money that was raised going to pay salaries and expenses rather than going to the kids, and so I told John that he should start his own foundation. So he did. And he got this woman, whom he had met when she worked for Make-A-Wish, to run it for him. That was actually my idea, which I later came to regret. She had just been let go from Make-A-Wish, but I had always seen her work really hard for them, so I just figured it was a personality conflict or something. She had a personality conflict, all right. *With me.* But that didn't boil up to the surface for a while.

Right after John formed the foundation, Jennifer and I organized a big fundraising dinner for it. We called it "Wives Gone Wild," and she and I hosted it with a few of her friends who were other basketball wives. We planned everything in just a few weeks, but it ended up being this amazing, huge extravaganza. We had it at the Horseshoe Casino and we sold tables for $5,000 each and served this fancy dinner to all of the guests. One of my friends had a connection with the country singer Clay Walker. He came and performed completely for free. He wouldn't even let us pay him for his gas. And he did it for Jennifer and me because he believed in our event, not because John Daly was some big famous golfer.

It was a huge success. We made around $150,000, and it was the only one of the fundraisers held for John's charity that ever made money like that. Then, after we'd done so much work and felt so good about what we'd accomplished, we found out that the money didn't even go to the charities we'd said we were going to help. I was really embarrassed about this because I'd gotten these two children's homes to give us all of these volunteers for the event, and they'd worked really hard. In exchange, they were supposed to get these big donations from the foundation. Well, John wouldn't let me have control of anything. He put the money wherever he wanted it to go. Anything I ever said, he went behind my back and said something different, and he made me look like this little dumb wife who had no say-so.

Well, I guess that's what I was, especially given what came next.

Hooters had been wanting to sponsor John for a while at that point, and they finally made him an offer in the spring of 2005. We were at the Masters, which is played in Augusta, Georgia, when we finally had it out about the whole thing.

"I don't want you to sign with them," I said. "I don't think it's good for you. This isn't what you need."

"But it's a ton of money," he said.

"We have a good thing going," I said. "Our system is working. We don't need their money. Their money is going to cost you a lot more money from other people in the long run. You're going to go down."

But he just couldn't say no to the money or the attention. Hooters had a big event to celebrate signing John to their sponsorship deal. My friend Alex was traveling with us, and she and I got all dressed up and walked from the bus to the Hooters restaurant where they were having the ceremony. When we got there and went to go through the door to watch John sign his contract, the police surrounded me.

"They said you can't be here," this policeman said.

"What?" I said. "Who?"

I couldn't believe it. We weren't fighting or anything. All I had said was that I was worried for him. And now, here he was turning his own wife away from one of the biggest moments in his career. The area was completely packed because it was the Masters and all of these people were watching all of this. It was really embarrassing.

But I didn't freak out or try to fight my way in there. I just stood real quiet, with tears pouring down my face. I didn't understand what he was doing or why. For once, I was too upset to make a scene.

And the cop wouldn't budge.

"I haven't done anything," I said.

"We got a call that said you were going to cause trouble up here," he said.

"No, not at all," I said. "I didn't get all dressed up and walk all the way over here to have any trouble."

I started to make a Plan B. Hootie & the Blowfish were playing at this park in town that night, and after the signing, we were all supposed to go over to the concert. So Alex and I were outside of the Hooters in this whole mess of people, and I called my contact at the show to make sure I could still get the passes from him.

"John's acting crazy," I said. "I just need to get the passes."

"Sherrie, he took the passes and told me not to give them to you," he said.

"Okay, no hard feelings," I said. "I know how John is."

Well, of course, now I really had to show John that he couldn't control me, no matter what he might think to the contrary. And when I got mad, that meant there was no stopping me.

"You know what?" I said. "We're not leaving. We're going into Hooters."

"Really?" Alex said. "How?"

"Just find a table of guys," I said. "Act like we know them, stand there, and order some beer."

Finally, the police said we could go into the Hooters if we wanted to, so we did, but we kept away from John and his trolls. There was a big cake and all of this stuff for the signing. John was in there, hanging out with all of his toothless, seventh grade–educated, hillbilly-ass buddies. And of course I'm sure they were all happy that they'd gotten him and me in a fight, so they could be VIPs at the big party at Hooters.

We did just like I planned. We buddied up to this table of guys and had some beers. Finally, John looked up and saw us in there. While I was sure he was watching, I took a beer and guzzled it to make him think I was having the best time, drinking and laughing and talking to these guys. I even turned to this one guy from the group and hugged him to make it look like we were friends.

"You look so familiar," I said.

I'm sure the guy was thinking: *I'll take this hug, but you're crazy, bitch.*

But I didn't care. I was getting into this whole scene that I'd created. Finally, when I was sure that John had no doubt in his mind that he couldn't keep me out of anywhere I wanted to be, or stop me from having my fun, I pulled Alex out of there.

"Come on, Alex, we're leaving," I said.

"How are we going to go?" she said.

"I've got a ride," I said. "Just come on."

We walked out the front door, and of course we were in these big heels, so that was about as far as we really wanted to walk that night.

"Okay, where's our ride?" she said.

"I don't have one," I said. "Just keep walking. I'll get us one in a minute."

The street was packed with people. And there were no cabs. We walked back down to the bus so I could gather my thoughts and come up with a strategy while John was still down there partying at the Hooters.

"Let's make a drink," I said.

So we made a drink from the bus's kitchen, and while we were sitting in the front lounge, I decided then and there that for once, even though John was trying to control me like he always did, I wasn't going to end up sitting on the bus crying like I had so many nights before. I was going to be a grownup and make my own decisions.

"Here's our plan," I said. "Every time you or any of my friends comes out on tour, he's so jealous, he just ruins the trip."

"He does, doesn't he?" Alex said.

"Yeah, he always creates this disaster, so that I don't ever have any fun."

It was weird but true: He didn't ever want me to have fun with my friends, even Alex, who John genuinely liked and was always happy to have travel with us. He would always get drunk and pass out, or tear the house up, or end up in an ambulance, so I'd have to give all my attention to him.

"But you know what?" I said. "I've brought you all the way to Augusta, and we left the kids at home and everything. I have a purse full of money. We are going to leave that son of a bitch, and we are going to have the best night we've ever had in our friendship. I promise you we are. We're not even looking back."

We got off the bus and walked across the street, and there was this police officer sitting there with this race car that was parked right across from the bus.

"Look," I said to him. "We're going out now. We're probably going to get drunk. When I come back to this bus at three in the morning, will you be here?"

"Yeah, I'm here all night," he said.

"Well, my husband is a real weird liar," I said. "So will you just please walk us over when we get back?"

"Sure," he said.

"If he causes us any trouble, I don't want him to say I did anything. He's nuts. And I'm real worried about it. I don't want to go to jail in Augusta, Georgia."

See, that's how well I knew John by that point in our marriage.

"No, I'll be here, and I'll take care of it for you," he said. "So y'all go and have a good time. Where are you going, anyhow?"

"We're going to walk over to that Hootie & the Blowfish concert," I said.

"Oh no, that's way over there," he said, pointing. "You can't walk there."

I think that was the year that someone had gotten shot or mugged or something at the Masters. There was like a crazy man loose—other than John, I mean—and so everyone was real jittery.

The cop turned and rounded up his two little buddies, who weren't much more than twenty years old. They were cops also, but they were off duty.

"We'll drop y'all off," they said.

"Are you sure you don't mind, really?" I said.

So we got in their big four-wheel-drive truck, and we decided we were going to take them with us and make good use of them that night.

Now, at the time, John had that evil witch working for him. She caused so much trouble in our marriage. And she should have been grateful too, since I was the one who'd told him to hire her after she left Make-A-Wish. But that's how it was: Everybody wanted to be close to him, and to do that, they felt like they had to push me away, and so they made up lies about me talking to other guys and stuff, just to get John and me into fights. Well, it turned out that she was backstage at the concert with him, and all up his butt. She's probably the one who took my passes away, as a matter of fact.

So we got over to the concert while the band was still playing, but we didn't have any tickets. And there were no tickets left to buy. It was sold out.

"Watch this, guys," I said. "I've got it."

Some people came by, and I got them to give me their stubs. Me and Alex and the two little cops used these broken-down ticket stubs to get ourselves in the gate. I knew John was looking for me, so I got us some drinks and then I led us over to the top of this hill where I was sure we'd be seen.

I turned to Alex and held my drink up to hers.

"You smile," I said. "Just smile. Like ha ha ha."

There was this really handsome guy standing on the hill near us. He was way cuter than the cops, so once again, I did the fake conversation thing with him until I made sure John had seen me. And then we were free to go out and really do it up.

Those little guys were so much fun. We took them to this bar where the cocktail waitresses carried trays full of test-tube shots.

I pulled a big wad of cash out of my purse.

"I'll take the whole tray," I said.

We were just drinking and partying and having the best time.

Near the end of the night, I knew exactly where we needed to go next. Supposedly, they always imported all of these high-class— well, if you can call them "high class"—strippers for the Masters every year. And this one club in Augusta was known as the place that had flown in all of these good-looking girls.

"Let's go there," I said.

"Really?" the guys said.

"Sure, because if we go in with y'all, they'll let us in," I said.

So we headed over there and went on in.

One of the guys stopped us before we went any farther.

"Well, you know, I do have this girlfriend who works here," he said. "Do you think we could make her a little jealous?"

"Of course we can," I said.

John wasn't in there, but it was better that way because we had such a good time. I came up with this big story about how these two little cops had to be our personal bodyguards because Alex and I were princesses from some foreign country, and we couldn't speak a word of English. Those guys told the strippers that, and they believed them and were basically waiting on us hand and foot. We'd make these noises like we were talking in another language, and then we'd write something down and show it to the guys. And the guys "translated" for us.

"They want something to eat," the one guy said.

We had these girls going across the street to this restaurant near there to get us food. We had the biggest time.

Finally, around four in the morning, the policemen drove us back to the bus in their truck. While we were driving back, I started thinking about how possessive and crazy John could be. We figured we'd been left behind for sure.

"He may not be there," I said. "But maybe he is."

We pulled up, and the bus was still there. I was so relieved. But I was hungry too. And now that I knew I wasn't stranded, I didn't want the fun to be over yet.

"Okay," I said. "Let's go to the Waffle House."

We went to get something to eat. And when we came back, the bus was gone.

No matter what all happened later, our wedding at the chapel at Bally's Las Vegas casino was a really beautiful day.

Thank God I've always had my parents to support me. And by the way, my dad doesn't smoke. But he does joke.

John and I
out on the town.

Living with John meant that I
never knew what to expect.
This was taken the day before
John said I stabbed him. I
caddied for him for eighteen
holes at the Stanford St. Jude
Championship and raised a
bunch of money for charity,
and we both had a great time.

John and I on a rare date night when I was able to convince him to actually get dressed up and take me out to dinner.

John and Little John, happy as can be.

Celebrate good times! The night John won the Buick Open we celebrated with Pat Perez and his now wife, Athena.

After I filed for divorce the first time in 2003, we reconciled in time for John to win the 2003 Callaway Golf Pebble Beach Invitational, which was the beginning of a comeback that lasted until 2005.

Not only was I thrilled to meet a legend like Merle Haggard, but he was as sweet as could be to Austin, which made me an even bigger fan. John said he'd never seen me go crazy over any celebrity like I did over Merle.

John with the boys at an LSU football game.

Tiger appeared to be a family man too. Look how sweet he was to Austin.

I met the President after walking eighteen holes and getting rained on. And so, of course, my White House picture has to be one of the worst in my life.

When John was feeling generous, he really was generous. Here I am with the Mercedes he gave me for my thirtieth birthday. Of course, he later smashed it. And when I took it in for repairs, they wouldn't give it back because they said the car didn't belong to me.

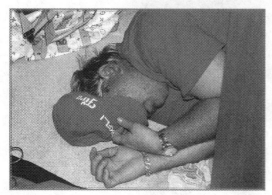

John had a dark side too, which I called JD. Here's JD, passed out in my closet after coming home wasted, trashing the house, and ripping up my clothes.

Living large in the Presidential suite at Bally's in Las Vegas on New Year's Eve, with me, Austin, John, and Little John.

John as a proud papa on Halloween, with Little John as a pumpkin and Austin as the Incredible Hulk.

Together as a family at Austin and Little John's christening.

This is one of my favorite pictures of John and Austin, who learned to love music and performing from John.

John and Austin relaxing in Reno.

Thanks to my friends Doc and Wendy for coming to Memphis and making my kids feel like they were still living in the fast lane, even without John, when we all got to hang out with Gene Simmons.

Like father, like son. Little John already has his dad's big swing. I think he could really go far in golf, if he chooses to play.

"Oh my God," I said. "What are we going to do?"

It was the Masters. There were no rooms in Augusta. But those little cops were so nice. They told us that the police always had a few rooms blocked off here and there for their undercover cops and other investigations and stuff. So they found us one of these empty rooms at the Days Inn. Mind you, we had no clothes. I had forgotten my cell phone on the bus when we were back there drinking. So the cops took us to a Kroger supermarket first, and we got some magazines, toothbrushes, some toothpaste, and just like anything we could buy at Kroger to spend the night with.

We had to share a bed, and by that time our clothes were so dirty and smoky that they were just too disgusting to sleep in. Well, Alex is like me—she doesn't wear any panties—so we were just like, *Okay, you stay over there and I'll stay over here.*

But that was such a fun night. We were still laughing in the morning, even though we were stranded, and we didn't know what we were going to do. Alex loves candy, so we had bought all of this candy at Kroger, and we were just lying in bed, eating candy and reading magazines until we could figure it out.

Alex was actually on the phone with my friend with the private jet, and he and his girlfriend were going to come get us. But then John called me on Alex's phone to apologize. And that witch who worked for him went ahead and moved me off of the bus and loaded up my car with all of my belongings and brought it to me at the Days Inn, like she couldn't wait to get rid of me. Now, Alex and I had just been planning to go to the Masters that day and have fun anyhow and not even worry about John. But the witch called and had our badges canceled. I know it was her, because John's not smart enough to think of something like that. And I think he was freaked out when he couldn't find me that night, but he wouldn't ever let on that he had feelings about anything, so he stayed away until he started feeling so bad that he had to call. Or maybe he just got to thinking, and he didn't want Alex and me to be on a road trip by ourselves with all of those clothes because he knew we might never come home again.

When we finally met up with the bus, I set things straight right away.

"All I've got to say is, whoever took my stuff off this bus had better get it back on," I said. "It'd better be back on there, and every shoe had better be in the same place."

So they just started hustling like busy bees, unpacking my stuff, making sure it was just like it had been. John and I made up, and we all ended up going to see Hootie & the Blowfish that night at this event called Monday After the Masters. Just like that, it was like nothing was wrong, and we all had a great time. That's how it always was. It was perfect or hell. Perfect or hell. There was nothing in the middle.

seven

WINNING BIG AND LOSING EVEN BIGGER

IT WASN'T LIKE I had a problem with Hooters in general. I even had pictures of my little boy with Hooters girls. So I didn't mind if, once a year during the Masters, John went to Hooters and signed autographs for an hour. That was no big deal.

But then when he signed his deal with Hooters, it turned into a whole different thing. When we went from city to city on the bus every week, instead of doing our little routine where we'd get into town, find the grocery store, and set ourselves up while we were there, he'd go to Hooters and strand me at some campground on the bus with both kids and no car.

And he didn't go and sign autographs for one hour anymore. He would start drinking, and they would bring him pitcher after pitcher of beer, and he wouldn't come home until after one o'clock in the morning. And this was when he had a seven or eight A.M. tee time to make.

And then John got this trailer to sell his merchandise from, and all of his buddies started coming along with us to drive the trailer and join him in this big, never-ending party. Well, that wasn't what I had signed up for when I married John. As much as I like to drink and have a good time, I'm a family person. I'm not going on the road three hundred days out of the year, and leaving all of my friends and family, and denying my children a normal childhood with friends and school, just so John could be out there on the road drinking, signing naked butts, and missing cuts. If he was going to make the cut and get down to business and play golf like he was supposed to, then I'd do this, no matter how challenging it could be. But I wasn't traveling all over the country to be on a drunk festival with him and all of these stupid hillbillies. It made me so mad, later on, when he said his wife wasn't supportive. Well, I'm sorry, but my ass will never be out at the Masters selling T-shirts with a tin can. I'm not saying I wouldn't do it for a charity or something like that, but not so John Daly could have more money to throw away on the slots.

Worst of all was when he would do these new Hooters outings. I would go to these things, and it was nothing but a total spectacle. He'd be drunk, with all these drunk Hooters girls hanging all over him and rubbing up against him at the tee box all day long. It was just very inappropriate behavior for a married man, even if that married man was John Daly. No one would have wanted their husband to be doing that. You know, signing titties, signing butts. I mean, I've got pictures where in Tampa he's got some girl—I don't even know if it was her tongue that was on his face or what, but it was ridiculous.

And that was just the stuff I saw. Even more than that, it was very degrading for me to have to go to tournaments after he'd been acting like a pig in front of all the other golfers and their wives, and everybody knew all about it but me. He still tried to pull off this whole different act when I was around, but it was getting harder and harder to pretend. I mean, I know that he was living wrong long before the Hooters girls came into our lives, but they definitely made his behavior even worse.

It got to the point where I felt like, if I saw him in one more picture with a Hooters girl, I was just going to blow. I was so over it. I was sick of those orange shorts. I hated the gross, tight T-shirts. Even the funky wings got me angry. I thought it was all trashy. I remember he tried to throw it at me once that Playboy sponsored Jay Don Blake; and his wife, Marci, who John knew I was close friends with, wasn't mad about that. No, Marci wasn't mad about it because Jay Don didn't go sit at the Playboy Mansion and drink and party with those girls all night long and have Playmates strutting around the golf course everywhere he went.

The final straw for me was when Hooters showed up at the golf course in Tampa and they set up a tent on the seventeenth hole. I was walking along with the other wives I was friends with, and all of a sudden, here were these Hooters girls with their titties flopping around everywhere, holding up these signs and screaming for

John. It was just nasty. I was so disgusted that I couldn't take it anymore. I walked off the course and went into the clubhouse. And then I got in my car and left.

"It's bad enough that he displays Hooters on his bag," I said. "But when I have to look at it like that, I'm done."

After that, we were at the U.S. Open in Pinehurst, which was held June 15 to 19, 2005. This was during the time when he was drinking and partying, and he played terribly. He had been up for an early tee time that morning, and we had our bus parked at the home of this really nice couple that John had gone to college with. I never met many of his friends that I liked before this, but this was a classy lady. She was a schoolteacher, and her husband was also really sweet.

After John was done playing, all the men got in one car and the women shared another, except for the caddie's girlfriend. Now, she and I had a history. I didn't like her to begin with, and then she had this habit of entering clubhouses and shamelessly saying, "Hi, I'm here with John. I'm here to play golf." And I would be totally embarrassed. First off, I would never be playing golf. And I would never be dressed like her or smelling like a pickled drunk. Her impersonation was straight out of *Single White Female* to me. But then I would feel sorry for her because she was like, "She thinks she's so much better than me. She never invites me anywhere. She and her friends are mean to me." But I didn't have a pass to get her where the wives went. She had a caddie pass. So out of the goodness of my heart, I would get her clubhouse passes. I would get her family passes and invite her to places and try to be nice to her so she'd feel like more than just the caddie's girl. But at the end of the day, she only wanted to go with the men anyhow.

Well, on this day, I didn't care about the arrangement because I didn't really want to be with the men, or with her, so I went with the schoolteacher and her sister, who everyone had called the Woopa Sisters since college. We girls decided to go eat sushi. We left the golf course at the same time that the men and the caddie's girlfriend got into their car to go to McDonald's. I knew John was in a bad mood because he had played really bad that day, but I figured John had his friends and a Big Mac coming, so what's the problem? I'd be back in no time. And I mean, the town square is so compact, you could throw a rock nearly to the house we were staying in. John had no reason to be jealous. I was going to be right down the street.

Well, when we returned to the house, no more than an hour later, the first thing I noticed was that the bus parked out front didn't have any windows. So I was like, *You stupid son of a bitch.* Here me and my kids were going to have to ride home covering ourselves with sheets so the broken glass wouldn't blow on us because he'd knocked everything out. This was like every other week. I was just over it. But I didn't say anything.

Well, I walked in the house to find the caddie's girlfriend preparing homemade salsa in the kitchen, and she started in with me.

"Sherrie, you know John had a really bad day today. You should have been here for him. He really needed you."

I'm thinking: *Oh no, you didn't just get into my business.*

So I just walked over to her.

"Look, talk to the hand," I said, and I pointed at her, really rudely. "Because me and my husband are none of your business. The best thing for you to do is to mind your own, find you some whatever it is, or just chop your little onions and peppers you got over there and leave me the hell alone."

I left her there to go find John on the back porch. I calmly took a seat in a chair beside him. And I didn't say anything about him tearing up the bus. I just acted like I didn't even know.

Well, the caddie's girlfriend came flying out the door, screaming.

"She's so mean to me! She's so mean to me!"

"Shut up, bitch," I said. "Chop chop."

She jumped over a little table and knocked me out of my chair, like flat on my back. Now, I've never been knocked out of a chair, and I've run my mouth plenty in my life at people a lot taller and bigger than me. She had me down on the ground, my shoulders pinned to the edge of the porch. She was trying to punch me in my face. So I put my leg up and started kicking her, and I pulled the back of her hair over. I was wildly punching her, and even though I was getting tired, I was afraid if I stopped punching her, she'd break my nose. And I was thinking, *Is somebody going to help me?*

Because what was my husband doing? Yelling encouragement—to the caddie's girlfriend.

"Kick her ass," he said. "Kick her ass."

I was like: *Oh my God, I'm in* The Twilight Zone.

It's like he wanted her to beat me up or something, because he was mad that I went to eat sushi instead of going to McDonald's with him.

Austin was in the backyard pool and saw that someone was on top of his mother, and John was clearly not helping because he was cheering her on. So Austin rushed over and started curb-stomping the caddie's girlfriend.

"Don't you hit my mamma!" he said.

She grabbed my baby's leg and bit it.

Now Austin was screaming. He got real mad and into the fight with us. Finally some of the other men, including her boyfriend, John's caddie, tried to break up the fight.

"Get her to let go of me!" she yelled. "Get her to let go of me!"

Finally they got us separated.

Afterward, I called my mom and debated if I should call the police, but I didn't want a police car over here. This was the U.S. Open. John had big sponsors then.

What made me the most furious was John's lack of help. I could not believe he had cheered on the caddie's girlfriend. Then he tried to lie and say he hadn't. But I was there. As for her, I should have called the police and had her arrested for attacking me in front of my kid. But then I thought, *No, I'm not doing anything.* But I told them, "Do not bring her back around me ever. She's not to come to any golf course. I don't want to see her face, ever, ever again." That was our agreement. And in the morning, I was planning to go to the police station and get a restraining order. But when we woke up in the morning, the police were already at the door. She had beaten me to the police station to make a report.

I went to the police station and told them what had really happened, but I still had to go to court a year later.

That July 21, a story ran in the *Florida Times-Union* that basically called John out on being the bad-living white trash that he was. Well, he didn't like that, so he sued them for defamation of character, a case he tried to get me involved in later.

Even when John won on the course, we couldn't count on things being good. On October 9, 2005, he played one of the best games of his career. It was at the American Express Championship, and he had a playoff with Tiger. He ended up coming in second, but still, that was the only playoff he ever had with Tiger, and he was really on that day. And he won $750,000. But like I said, with the money came the problems. There was this old couple from Seattle who were hanging around at that time, and they acted so Christian, and they always wanted John to call them Mom and Dad, and yet they were always trying to hook him up with whores in Vegas and go gambling. I even heard the husband leave a message for John one time telling him he had some girls for John at the Pussy Palace. The lady, especially, liked to gamble, and she wanted John to go to Vegas. And this was at a time when John had just been to the Wynn casino and lost a bunch of money, so we did not need to go to Vegas and lose any more. The money we'd just won was already spoken for, as it needed to go to taxes and other bills. But of course there was no talking sense to John once he'd made up his mind to do something.

"Let's go to Vegas," he said.

So we did. He drove out of the parking lot after coming in second after the WGC-American Express Championship and we headed straight to Vegas. The lady convinced him to go back to the Wynn, even though I thought it was a bad idea.

"That's the lose," I said about the Wynn. "I don't want to gamble there. If we're going to Vegas, let's just go to Bally's. We win at Bally's."

When it comes down to my karma and good luck, I wanted to go to where we did good instead of staying at the fancy place. And I loved Rick Zeller, the casino host at Bally's. I mean, he and his wife were two of twelve people at my wedding. To go and stay at the Wynn felt like cheating on them. But John wouldn't listen.

"She's got us set up at the Wynn," he said.

I had a bad feeling the whole time we were checking in. Even though it was *the* place, and it was beautiful and the shopping was wonderful, to me, staying there wasn't worth whatever he was fixing to lose in the casino that day. We could have just rented a room somewhere for five grand.

They gave us the room of all rooms. We had our own private pool. And everything was the royal treatment. Everyone knew us there, and the butlers came in to get us all set up, and they sent a babysitter up for the kids so I could go down and meet John in the casino. I looked like holy hell, so I took a shower and got dressed, but not in anything fancy, just some jeans and heels, or something like that. It couldn't have taken me much more than an hour to finish getting ready.

I went downstairs and headed over to the VIP area. And there was this hallway that went by the high-limit area and the high-limit slot machines. I walked through, looking for John, and he was coming toward me. He just looked at me, and I couldn't tell what was wrong because he'd played so well and had such a good day.

"I just lost almost a million fucking dollars," he said.

"What?"

"I just lost almost a million fucking dollars."

"Oh my God," I said. "How?"

It literally had been an hour and a half. We just stood there in silence, and he looked like he wanted to die. It had basically been one of the biggest golf matches of his life and he'd just lost nearly every dime of it. I still didn't get it.

"How did you lose that much?"

"I was playing a five-thousand-dollar slot machine," he said.

Well, with those, each pull was $5,000, which adds up fast.

And it didn't stop there, either. Even with some wins at Bally's, John lost $1.65 million in less than five hours that day.

By the end of it all, I was thinking: *Oh my God. Oh my God.*

But being the supportive, positive person that I am, I just started laughing. I figured, *Well, we can either laugh or we can cry.* He looked at me like I was crazy.

"I just lost everything," he said. "And I've got to pay taxes on that."

"Let's just act like today never happened," I said. "Let's just act like you didn't win that money. And let's just move on to the next thing. Let's not ever talk about this again. It's over. It's done."

He looked like he couldn't believe what I was saying.

"I guess what I'm going to do is go shopping," I said.

And, oh my gosh, did I! It was almost like work. The Wynn comped me $5,000 for every $100,000 he spent. And I figured I had to get everything I could from that casino because I knew what we had just lost. I went into my favorite store at the casino, and I'm sure I bought the kids $10,000 worth of clothes. Literally one of everything—the James Perse, the Rock and Republic jeans, the motorized Razor vehicles—everything they had at that store, the Wynn shipped to my children. So at least my kids were walking around looking like little pimps, even though John and I were broke. And of course, I got myself one of everything, I got my mom one of everything. I didn't know what else to do, so I just got in as much retail therapy as I could.

Well, of course, the story of our rise and fall hit the papers the next day, and that made it even worse. It was all over, and I just felt like we looked so stupid. I mean, I had seen John lose a lot of money in one night before. And I know this will sound totally insane to anyone who's never lived like this, but I had kind of gotten used to it, especially because we had so much money coming in from his appearances and sponsorships. Anyhow, it was different to lose the money $100,000 at a time, at three different casinos or something like that, when it didn't add up to $1.65 million. Sometimes we went to Caesars and he lost $150,000, and then we went over to Bally's and lost another $150,000. But then we went back to Caesars and won $300,000. It was always an up and down, rollercoaster kind of thing. And if we were there for a couple of weeks, we usually ended up not having lost that much by the time we left, especially when you figured that we went to Vegas and lived like kings and queens for two weeks, staying at the Elvis Presley suite at the Hilton, with nannies and butlers taking care of everything and the kids buying every toy at FAO Schwarz. Maybe we were down $200,000, but in the end, it probably wouldn't have cost too much less than that if we'd paid for it all out of our pockets. But $1.65 million? That was serious. Even John knew that was serious, and he didn't ever seem to get fazed by much.

Of course, if I'd known what was coming for us in the next few months, I would have been glad that we'd at least had a Vegas vacation together—even if it turned out to be a bad one—while we still could.

eight

"YOU'LL WANT TO WEAR PANTIES HERE," OR, MY TIME ON THE INSIDE

DURING THAT WHOLE TIME, my family was still facing legal problems. My dad's lawyers wanted him to take a deal, but he would have had to say he was guilty, and he wasn't going to say anything that made it seem like he was involved in any way with dealing drugs. I mean, he's old school. Like if he ever had cause to talk about it, which he doesn't, he would probably call pot a "marijuana cigarette." Anyhow, he was warned that the prosecutor was probably going to go after his wife and daughter if he didn't make the deal, but we certainly weren't going to have him compromise himself, even if it would have made our lives easier. So my dad ended up having to serve two and a half years, and my mom got five months for making deposits for my dad's car dealership. I was devastated. Not only was it scary and hard for me to think about my parents in prison, but my family is real close. I relied on my parents for everything, especially as my life with John got more and more chaotic. They watched the kids for us when we couldn't take them on the road, and sometimes even John's daughters from his earlier marriages. They loaned us money when John lost all of ours gambling and we were about to come up short on something we owed. And even more important, I knew if things ever got really crazy with John, they would be there for me. And now, suddenly they weren't.

Luckily, we had so many wonderful people in our lives. I can't say enough good things about our sponsors, 84 Lumber, who were so supportive when everything happened with my parents. From the time John signed with them, they were so good to my family. We always went up there and stayed with them. Mr. Hardy had two young girls. They would sometimes travel with us to tournaments. It was a very close relationship, like family—which makes sense, since family always came first for them, as a way to manage their business and a way to live. And his older daughter, Maggie, who helped him run things, was just the sweetest. John and I were in Hawaii when I found out about my parents going to prison. And when we got back, we went up to 84 Lumber for an outing. I sat outside the bus and I cried for so long. I mean, I was crying uncontrollably for days. Maggie came to the bus to cheer me up with all these gifts, including a Harry Winston watch. And on the day my dad and mom went to jail, John gave me a really big diamond cross necklace. Of course, it was the kind things that John and Maggie both said to me during this time that meant the most to me, but I've always been big on symbols, and those gifts were important because they helped me to remember the good in my life during one of my hardest experiences.

Now, I had narrowly avoided going to jail that year myself. I had filed for an appeal. When you get an appeal, you have to get something called a stay, which allows you to stay out of jail during the appeal process. Otherwise, they could decide to send you to jail during the appeal. Well, I was in Palm Springs, sitting outside the clubhouse, and I got this call telling me that I hadn't gotten my stay and that I had to go to jail the next day. So I got on the phone and literally called everyone I could think of who might be able to help me with this. Finally, I got the idea to call Bill Clinton because of how nice he'd been when I'd met him at that golf outing. I don't even remember how I got his number; I think I called the White House switchboard and then I called some number in New York. I'm really good with the telephone, so I just got on the phone and stayed there until I got Bill Clinton on the line. I explained the situation and that I felt like I'd been done dirty because there was this one guy who was telling a lot of lies about me and my family. Now, I know, just because I didn't understand that what I was doing with those deposits was wrong in the eyes of the law, ignorance doesn't excuse me. But they also filled in spots and made up stuff too, especially where my dad was concerned.

"Is there anybody you can call?" I said. "I don't know, in the FBI or whatever?"

He told me that he didn't trust anybody, but he wished I'd called him from the beginning. Even though there was nothing he could really do for me, he said he would have helped me find an attorney that might have done more for my case.

"We spent a total of $450,000 on attorneys," I said. "I thought there was justice."

He sat there for like thirty minutes and talked to me while I told him everything that had gone on with my dad. He was just so nice.

Luckily, I ended up getting a stay the next morning. I'm sure he didn't have anything to do with that, since he wasn't even in office at the time, but I'll always appreciate his kindness. And I was free from worrying about going to jail, at least for a little while.

Of course, living at my house gave me plenty of other stuff to worry about, especially that year. Ever since John signed with Hooters his drinking got worse and worse. And even the good times were fleeting. For my thirtieth birthday that October, John bought me an '06 Mercedes SL 65. We're talking a $200,000 car here. It was just gorgeous. Of course, that didn't last long. By the time the holidays rolled around, he was just a wild man. My best friend Gail invited me out to a holiday party, and when I decided to go, John became his usual insanely jealous self. Mind you, this was a *church party*, and I think I was home by nine-thirty that night. Well, that was enough time for him to take one of the boys' Razor scooters and use it to smash up my Mercedes. He dented all four sides, broke out all the windows, and left the scooter sticking out of the back window. It came to something like $30,000 worth of damage. It was like anytime he got scared I might leave him, even when I just went out for a couple of hours, this whole insane domino effect would go off in his brain. He would decide that I was not going to be able to go, at which time he usually tried to get me arrested. Or that if I did go, I wasn't going to leave with anything. This night, he took care of the latter. He took all of the jewelry he had bought me, plus some pieces I'd been given by other friends—we're talking Rolexes, Harry Winston watches, and some things that really meant a lot to me, like the cross he gave me when my mom went to jail—and smashed them all with a hammer. It was something like $300,000 worth of jewelry. All gone.

John always liked to keep me on my toes, even when it came to the good stuff. In January of 2006, his first reality show was about to air, and he did a big media tour for that. We went to New York, and he was on the *Today* show. We had left Little John at home, but Austin was sitting on his lap while he was on camera and I was just kind of watching from backstage. They started talking about Hooters.

"I've decided I'm not going to be with Hooters this year," he said. "I'm dropping Hooters because it's not good for my marriage, and my wife really doesn't like it."

I couldn't believe what I was hearing, but I thought that was a very big thing that he did, and I was so happy. This was one of the moments that reminded me of why I stayed with him through the rest of it. He could be sincere, and sometimes he would try. And I know that he had so many demons and so many battles, but I felt like he really didn't want to lose his marriage or his family.

Of course, by the time we got back in the car, Hooters was calling. They were trying to double his contract. And they wanted to talk to me. Now, at the same time, John was being courted by Stanford Financial, back when Stanford was big. My friend Angela's sister worked for them, and they were trying to give John a huge sponsorship. But instead of dating them, he was kissing the Hooters ass all the time, just hanging out drinking and being a fool.

"Sherrie," the guy from Hooters said. "This is just business. These girls, they're not out to mess with John. Do you really want to pass up all that money?"

"Yes," I said. "I do not want your money. It's not good for us. I don't like Hooters. I don't think it's a good image for John."

The guy kept trying to offer more money, to do anything to convince me.

"Whatever it is, we don't want your money," I said. "We have two houses now we don't see. We can't take care of our cars. We don't need the money. Please leave us alone."

But John just couldn't leave Hooters alone. It was not surprising, given the amount of money they were offering him, and the fact that he was a compulsive gambler, sex addict, and alcoholic—especially if it meant taking a dig at me. I think it was a week or so later when John had lost a bunch of money at the casino, and he was mad at me for something. I don't even remember what it was. I was probably bitching about one of his girlfriends or his drinking or his gambling. There was plenty for me to get on him about around then.

So he went behind my back and re-signed with them.

He thought he was getting me back, and I got mine, all right.

Now, clearly I'm no saint, but I do have a couple of rules of behavior that I try to stick by. I don't swear to God or use God's name in vain. I don't say "pussy." That's two of my things that I don't do. But when John signed with Hooters again, I walked through our house, just shrieking like a banshee.

"I swear to God, as long as you have Hooters on your shirt, I will never watch you play a hole of golf again. I will never be on the golf course. I'm done."

Well, I was right about that. The day after that, I got this message saying that I had lost my appeal, and I was supposed to have been in jail two days before. Now, I thought I had won my appeal, so I was really upset when I heard this. Then I started laughing. I guess God had really made me eat those words, because I sure didn't go watch John play golf. I couldn't: I was in jail for the next five months.

The sad truth, though, is that I needed a break from John. He had put me through so much hell by the time I went away that at least this was some peace. John was in California. We had money then. And I don't know if there's really a proper etiquette for how to behave when your wife gets sent to jail. But it might seem like he would have chartered a private plane, come home, seen me, and taken me to jail, and then gone back to California. But no, the last contact I had with him was by phone.

"I can't leave," he said. "I talked to Bud, and they've got a plane that's going to come and take you."

"But I want my friends to go with me," I said. "Can the plane take them too and then bring them back to Memphis?"

"No, Sherrie, the plane's got to go to Pittsburgh right after it drops you off."

Thanks a lot. Well, like I said, John wasn't the first man in my life to take me places on a private plane. I called my friend, who'd already said I could use his plane. I explained everything and he told me he would take me and get whatever I wanted on the plane for the trip. I never told John this, actually. Alex and I said that this other guy who had this little old propeller plane had brought me to jail with just her for company. But, really, we took my friend's Learjet, and Gail and our other friend Leslie came too. And all of us drank vodka the whole way, and I took a few Valiums too, for good measure. And I needed them. When we landed near the jail, I started freaking out.

It's funny, the things you worry about at a time like that.

"I'm not going to be able to eat any fried chicken in there," I said.

So the pilots made a call for me.

"Can we get her some Kentucky Fried Chicken brought to the airport?"

They got me Kentucky Fried Chicken, and we all got in the cab. Everyone was crying, even the pilots. I swear. So we got to the prison, and it had this really tall, razorblade barbed-wire fence, and there were men screeching obscenities out the window. We were all standing in a row in this empty parking lot and everybody was screaming and crying, me worst of all. And this little security truck came up to us.

"I can't go!" I screamed. "I can't go!

"She can't go!" all of my friends screamed.

The security guy looked at us and nearly busted out laughing.

"Y'all are at the wrong place," he said. "This isn't where she's staying. She's staying over there."

He pointed across the way at this little bitty schoolhouse that looked like an old gym. There was no security wire. There was no fence. The doors weren't even locked. We all let out the biggest sigh of relief.

I was still anxious, and I knew I needed to be calm for this, so I popped one more Valium. Luckily, the guards were really nice.

When I checked in, they went through this whole stack of routine paperwork. One guard assigned me my job washing pots and pans in the kitchen. And then another guard asked me a bunch of questions to make sure they gave me the right size uniform, until they came to a question that brought us up short.

"What size panties?" he asked.

"I don't wear panties," I said.

"You'll want to wear panties here," he said. "This is some rough polyester."

"Okay, small, I guess," I said.

When he gave me the small panties, they were huge.

But honestly, that was one of the worst problems I faced in there, so it really wasn't that bad. No one threatened me or gave me a hard time, or even gave me too much attitude, really. After I had my job washing pots and pans for a while, they switched me to working as a baker, which I liked because I made a lot of friends by sneaking off and baking birthday cakes for the other inmates, and I could eat all of the fresh-baked dinner rolls I wanted. And I had plenty of free time, which I spent sunbathing in the yard. Mostly, I was just bored. In fact, it would have almost been a nice vacation if my two baby daddies weren't so vindictive and mean. I swear, I acquired some real perspective with all that time I had to sit in there and think. And what it comes down to is that I don't care anything about the jewelry that was smashed or the money that was lost. But I will do anything for my children and my family and friends, and without them, I'd be lost.

Austin's dad tried to get custody of him while I was gone. When I went to jail, Austin was only six, so it was obviously very upsetting for him. At first, I had thought that he was going to go live with Mr. Hardy from 84 Lumber and his family, because Austin was really close with their two little daughters. That whole family was so sweet during this time. They sent their plane to pick Austin up, and the whole thing was full of stuffed animals and toys, and they brought him to their house in Pittsburgh. He was really happy there, and they were going to put him in school with their kids and everything. But I couldn't get his father, whom I used to call the sperm donor because of how little he chose to be involved in Austin's life, to agree to it. And then he started with this whole custody bullshit. He had never been around, ever, so that just put me over the edge. To make matters even worse, I had no way to call anybody to make sure my lawyer was fighting his attempt at custody. We were only given three hundred minutes of phone time a month, and I couldn't even get my attorney on the phone. But this one guard ended up being so nice to me; he let me use his cell phone to call my mom, who had finished her jail time the previous year, and she was able to get one of my attorneys to work everything out. But until that was settled, it was about to give me a nervous breakdown. Once I knew Austin was safe, I was okay about everything else.

Except for John. In the interviews he did during this time, he tried to act like he was so sad that his wife was gone. He wasn't sad. He was partying. His ex-wifey number three was there on the scene as soon as I left. I mean, I never knew what really went on with the two of them, but given what went on between him and pretty much every other woman he ever looked at, I can only imagine. Which, at this point, as far as I'm concerned, they can all have each other.

Now, I knew better than anyone else that John's schedule was very demanding and that he was really busy and had to travel constantly. It was my life for a long time too. But from January to June of 2006, while I was in jail in Kentucky, he passed through the area at least three times, to go play in a tournament at Myrtle Beach, and to go to all of these different places. He only stopped to see me one time. For two hours. He wasn't even playing most of the time when I was there, but he didn't even come to visit.

And this was someone who maybe should have been a little more sympathetic to my situation. He was the one who had insisted I talk to the FBI when they'd come to the bus one day the previous year to investigate my case, even though I'd wanted to have a lawyer present. Maybe if I'd waited to make a statement, like I'd wanted to, the whole thing would have gone down differently. Regardless, it's not like John was some perfect person himself. He could have so easily ended up in jail more times than I could count: he's bounced checks at casinos for hundreds of thousands of dollars; he's destroyed property; he's verbally and physically attacked at least two of his wives, including me; he's driven drunk. And if he had gone to prison, I would have been there every chance I had, with a picnic basket in hand, trying to make the best out of a bad situation, just like I always did. And he knew that, but he never stopped to think about me at all.

The one time he did come and see me, it was a weekend when my mom and friends were all there too, so I barely even got the chance to talk to him, and he only stayed for two hours before he rushed on out of there.

But I was always a dummy where he was concerned, so I never gave up hope. Every week, I would get dressed up and just sit there, waiting for a visit from him that never came. And to get dressed there was a really big deal. I was working with a little hair dryer that was probably twenty years old, and I was trying to straighten my hair with some product that, I don't even know what it was. It was just bad. But at least it worked better than nothing. Anyway. I would go to all of this trouble, and put on my Wet N Wild makeup and try to look pretty for my husband. And I did look good. I mean, I sure looked a lot less stressed while I was in there than I did when I was at home with him.

And there were all these poor ladies in there with me, and their husbands, in their raggedy cars that probably could barely make it up the hill, with all of their little kids loaded in the back, they never missed a day coming to see their wives. This one old man would even sit in the parking lot a day ahead because he was so excited for his visit. I mean, everyone else did what it took to see their wives, and they had it a lot harder than John and I did. I mean, we were like *Lifestyles of the Rich and Famous* compared to them.

So I would think if they could make it for a visit, John could surely make it to see me. And I'd be standing there, thinking: *He's coming. He's coming.*

But he never came but that once.

And I could just imagine all of the other women thinking: *She doesn't even have a husband. He's divorcing her.*

Usually I had no visitors whatsoever because as much as I was overjoyed to see my mom and my friends, I didn't like them to bring the kids too much. Little John was staying with my mom, and the first time he came to see me, he was barely old enough to walk, and at the end of the visit he looked at me like: *Okay, come on, Mom.*

I couldn't leave. And it just killed me. So it was easier for them not to come.

Except for on Mother's Day. That was the one time when it really meant a lot to me to see them. So all of my friends came and brought Austin with them. Of course, John had Little John that weekend and he wouldn't let them bring Little John along. And not because he had him out of town or had anywhere else to be or anything; instead of coming to see me, John brought Little John to the golf course and watched his greens grow or whatever it was he did over there.

So it's probably no surprise that, when my 150 days in the pokey were finally done, John didn't come to pick me up from jail, either. That's okay, though. My friends at 84 Lumber took good care of me, as always. Maggie and Joe Hardy sent their plane to come and take me away. It was completely packed with every luxurious spa product you could imagine, like Brown Sugar, and all of the other really good stuff. And there was shrimp, lobster, steak, and all of this other wonderful, fancy food to eat. And, of course, champagne and vodka, which I appreciated since I was definitely ready for a drink—or five—right about then. And, on top of all that, Maggie gave me this huge, gorgeous 84 Lumber necklace. I was happy enough just to be free, and then all of this was just absolute heaven after the polyester jumpsuits and Wet N Wild. I did do one thing that was a little naughty. I was supposed to go straight home for house arrest, but instead, I went to the 84 Lumber spa at Nemacolin. No one ever found out. But even if I had gotten in trouble, it would have been totally worth it. Best massage. Ever.

nine

THE "GOOD TIME" GIRL
SURVIVES HOUSE ARREST

Aᶠᵗᵉʳ ᵐʸ ᵖʳⁱˢᵒⁿ ˢᵉⁿᵗᵉⁿᶜᵉ, I sat at home for five months on house arrest, and John was present two times during those 150 days. When he wasn't home, I barely heard from him. Other people were calling the house, though. During one of John's brief visits, a girl he had been with called the *house* phone and asked for him.

"Yeah, let me get him for you," I said.

I went and found John in the other room and handed him the phone.

"Um, John, somebody wants to talk to you," I said. I had it on speakerphone, so I could hear the conversation too.

"Hi, John, it's Kelly," she said.

"I don't know her," John said to me.

"He doesn't know you," I said, into the phone, to Kelly.

"Oh, thanks for remembering me, John," she said to both of us.

I was getting to the point where pretty much nothing surprised me in terms of what John was capable of, and I really didn't have any more expectations about him being the husband I had hoped for when we first got married. I hadn't given up on our marriage because I still considered it a sacred, till-death-do-you-part vow, even if he clearly didn't, but let's just say I'd redefined my expectations. And I was okay with that. I really was. I knew I had a good life, in many ways, and I still had moments with John that were surprisingly nice and could keep me going. But the one thing I had absolutely no tolerance for was when his bad behavior impacted the kids. They were, and are, my number-one priority, and since he was Little John's dad and Austin's stepdad, he was supposed to feel the same way. Unfortunately, in John's world, there was only room for one person to come first: John, of course.

While I was under house arrest, Little John was scheduled to undergo ear surgery. I told John about the procedure, which was a big deal that was being done in an outpatient hospital, and it involved having our child put under anesthesia while tubes were inserted into his ears. I had been alone with Little John once before following a procedure that had involved anesthesia, and it had been horrible. Something about the way small children react to the drugs they give them is really harsh, and he had gone wild when he came to and I had to restrain him. The nurses couldn't believe I didn't have anyone there to help me. So I'd told John all of this and that I'd need his help. Well, John had other ideas. The night before the surgery, he did one of his disappearing acts. He was there at the house, and then I looked up and he was gone, without having said anything to me.

I called him, and at least he answered his phone this time.

"Are you not coming to Little John's ear surgery?" I said.

"No, you don't want me there."

Well, I had asked him to be there. What did I have to do, send him a written invitation? The bottom line was that he wanted to go to a University of Arkansas football game instead. So he didn't come home, and he wasn't there to help me.

Luckily the procedure went well, and I was fine without him there. But then, when Little John got home from the hospital, he had a fever, and I was worried about it. So I called John back to see what he thought I should do. He was on his bus when he picked up his phone. I was explaining what was going on, but I kept hearing this strange sound on the other end of the line, so I stopped talking. I don't even know how to describe it—and this is real nasty—but I heard the sloshing and slobbering of a blow job being given. I swear I could hear someone with him.

"What are you doing?" I asked.

He tried to pretend like nothing was going on.

I know I probably shouldn't have been, but I was stunned. I was thinking: *Surely he wouldn't, after his kid just got out of surgery, and he's home running a fever.*

So I decided to find out for myself. Now, I'd hired this detective earlier in the year, because I obviously knew John was cheating and I wanted evidence to prove it. But that night I couldn't get the detective over there, so my friend's nanny went and stalked outside the bus with a video camera. When I knew she was all set up outside, I called John back and confronted him.

"John, I know that you're on the bus with someone," I said. "I can hear it. You might as well just come off the bus because I've got a detective there who saw the girl go on the bus with you. And I've got the tag numbers off every car in the lot."

Okay, the detective part was a lie. But that nanny was a good sleuth, and the license plate part was true. We knew it was this ex-girlfriend of John's that he used to sleep with while he was married to ex-wifey number three. That trashball's car was parked right there by the bus.

John still tried to deny it. But I wouldn't let him get away with it this time.

"That slut's on the bus," I said. "And you need to just come off."

So he did. He thought if he came off the bus and he came on home, that I would let the whole thing go. Now, does that sound like me? No way. I was pissed. I told the nanny to stay right there because I knew the girl would have to leave the bus eventually. So about twenty minutes after John left, she finally came off the bus. And we've got footage of all of that on tape.

Now, John didn't know that part of the story, so as far as he was concerned, I had believed his lies and he had gotten away with the whole thing. But he's so stupid that he ended up giving me good reason to be suspicious, even if I hadn't known that anybody was there with him in the first place. When he walked in the door, I noticed that he was wearing his shirt inside out.

"Why'd you turn your shirt inside out?" I asked.

"I pissed on it," he said.

I could not make this stuff up if I tried.

"You pissed on your shirt?" I said. "Since you were on the bus, where we have a whole wardrobe for you, wouldn't you have thought to put on a different shirt, instead of just turning the piss shirt inside out?"

He didn't have a good answer for that. And I had even less respect for him than ever. I mean, who would think to say something like that about themselves? It's just gross. Not that that was surprising, coming from John. I mean, it was not uncommon for him to get so drunk in those years that he pissed the bed. So why not piss his shirt too?

I was under house arrest, so I couldn't leave our home. John was nowhere to be found. And when he was around, he was eroding our marriage even further day by day. There was just one thing for me to do to make myself feel better: I shopped the whole time I was stuck there like that. One day I bought thirty-six pairs of shoes over the phone, all in one go, from my favorite store in the whole world. It's called Gregory's and it's at the Galleria Mall in Dallas. Now, I first went there when I was twenty-one, and I bought my first pair of Donald Pliner shoes there. And I'd been going there at least once a year ever since, so I was good friends with the owner, Larry. And after John and I got married, when we would travel through there, we would go to the store together. I remember when a PGA tournament came to Texas, and Larry had heard that I had been indicted. So he waited until I came into the store, and he couldn't have been nicer.

"I had some issues with the feds myself," he said. "And I had to go to jail. I just wanted to tell you that I've been thinking about you and worried about you."

And so, when I was out on the road, I called him.

"Send me a box," I'd say.

And he'd take all of the new styles in my size and he'd pile them into a big box and ship them to me.

Now, after John got up to this latest round of bad behavior, and while his wife was stuck at home under house arrest no less, I figured that I deserved something a little extra special to make up for it.

"Send me a lot of boxes," I told Larry on the phone. "Send me as many boxes as they have in my size. Send me everything."

I think I spent $16,000 on shoes altogether. And when they arrived at the house, I couldn't resist letting John know that I was getting my payback. I modeled each and every pair for him.

"Do you like this, John?" I would say.

And then I'd put on another pair of equally fabulous shoes.

"Do you like this, John?" I would say again.

And of course, he knew there was only one answer when he was in trouble.

"Yeah, sure," he said. "I like everything."

The best thing about Larry, though, is that he's been as loyal to me as I've been to him over the years. Since John and I split up, and I've been poor, he always gives me a chance to get the sale stuff first. He'll actually mail sale items to me before he puts them on display in his store. And he never says anything to make me feel embarrassed or anything. Rich or poor, I always get treated well by him.

If it wasn't bad enough to be under house arrest, during this time I had to fly back to Pinehurst to go to court to face the civil suit for the fight I'd had with the caddie's girlfriend the previous year. I took Gail with me for moral support, and from day one we did not fit in. First of all, it was like they had never seen a black person before. We couldn't believe some of the looks we got. So the whole town was spooky and Gail was freaked out. I had to give her a Valium just to calm her down.

I wore these sweet pink shoes with bows on them and this nice pink suit to court. I looked so innocent, which I still felt I really was, since that woman attacked me while my husband egged her on. The caddie's girlfriend showed up, looking like a bum off the street, but she got up there on the stand and started boo-hooing. I went up there and they asked me the questions, and I told the truth and said that I was protecting myself. And John and all of his friends actually took my side and submitted testimony for me that said she had started it. I was relieved about that, because it seemed like whenever John and I were having marital problems, he was always trying to get me arrested, like he wanted to make sure I couldn't enjoy myself if he couldn't have me. But at least this time he was reasonable. I'd say it was the least he could do, since he'd encouraged her. Anyhow, I was sure I'd won. Then they said something about being guilty. I turned to Gail.

"Are they talking about me or her?" I asked.

And so we asked my attorney.

"No, you," he said.

I wanted to appeal but my attorney didn't think it was a good idea, since I had a criminal record and he figured I was unlikely to win anyhow. As restitution, they expected me to pay her damages, even though she'd jumped on me and tried to break my nose. I didn't pay it and I'm not planning to pay it.

Finally, partway through my house arrest, I got to go out for

my "good time," which is what they call the outings they let pris-
oners take as a reward for good behavior. My friend Hagmire,
who owns the company Limo Express, brought this limo over.
The usual suspects—Gail and Angela and I—plus a few others all
piled in.

"I want to go to Beale Street," I said, enjoying my freedom.
"I want some action."

How we drank as much as we did in such a short time, I don't
even know, but we just started doing Jell-O shots, drinking vodka
this, vodka that, champagne, and we were good and drunk by the
time we even got to the city, which is about twenty minutes from
my house at Southwind.

We went straight to Coyote Ugly on Beale Street, and we
continued drinking. Well, it didn't take very long before Angela
and I climbed right up on the bar. I had my leg up in the air with
the ankle bracelet for my house arrest on full display. I had a
whole fan club, loving the ankle bracelet, and I was working it. I
was so happy to be out with my friends and to be having fun for
once. I'm more than sure we were dancing to "Cotton-Eyed Joe,"
or some other country song, and we were just going wild. The
only problem was that my sandals were smooth-soled, and I kept
slipping, so I took them off. But there was a rule against that, and
the bartender got mad.

"You have to put your shoes back on," she said to me.

"But I'm going to fall off," I said.

As soon as I put my shoes back on, I did. I slipped and fell right
off the other side of the bar, back to where the bartenders work.
Luckily this waitress literally caught me in the air as I went over
and set me down on the ground. I was laughing so hard. I had to

walk all the way around to get back to the other side of the bar, but it was all part of the adventure.

We stayed out as late as we could, but my house arrest officer, Mr. Shaw, had given me a curfew I had to meet. Finally, we got back into the limo with just enough time to get me home, down to the minute.

But I wasn't quite ready for my night to be over yet.

"I've got to have some chicken," I said.

I don't know why, but I'm always wanting chicken, especially when I've been drinking. For some reason, I always crave Kentucky Fried Chicken.

So Hagmire turned the limo around and started driving me to KFC. My sensible friends did not like this one bit, and they all started yelling.

"You can't get her any chicken!"

"I'm getting her the chicken," he said.

"No, she's got to go home, or she's going to get in trouble with Mr. Shaw!"

"I don't care," he said. "We're getting the chicken."

So we were late, but I got my chicken. And Mr. Shaw didn't get too mad.

Finally, my house arrest was over too. And I was a free woman.

I wouldn't say that I was a different person after that, but something had definitely changed inside of me. All of a sudden, John was back in the picture, and he wanted things to be like they had been before, with me traveling on the road with him and doing what he wanted us to do when we were home. My first thought was: *I'm not being a Stepford Wife anymore.*

I figured this Stepford Wife had sat in jail and at home for a combined total of three hundred days. And she basically only saw her husband for two days and two hours out of those three hundred days, during which time she had to share his attentions with the other women he was also screwing. And, after all of that, he thought he was going to come back on the scene now and run the roost?

No thank you. I'm the boss now.

There was no way he was ever telling me what to do, ever again. For years, he had controlled every aspect of my life. My reality had been shaped around his travel schedule, his jealousy, and his bad moods. He had told me not to talk to this person. And not to talk to that person. By this point in our marriage, I never went over to my friends' houses because it just wasn't worth it. When I did, I was always so worried about making him mad. And even all of that wasn't enough; I still had to be walking on eggshells because he was so unpredictable. And I had never complained. I had been so devoted to making my marriage work and keeping John happy, that I'd done whatever it took, no matter how insane it might seem by other people's standards. But it hadn't worked anyhow. Nothing I did was enough to make him into a reasonable, rational person. And by then I was starting to get that he was so insanely jealous because of what his own bad self was doing. Well, he could be as jealous as he wanted.

The way I figured it, I was an adult woman now. I had done my time. I had been 150 days in jail, then 150 days with Mr. Shaw. And I was going to do just what I wanted to do. After that, I gave John a dose of his own medicine. All of those little disrespectful digs he'd always taken at me: I started doing them to him now, like not answering my phone, or going out whenever and wherever I felt like it, as long as my mom or someone I trusted could stay with the kids. If I got good and ready to go out and eat at a restaurant and he didn't want to go—which he never wanted to—I had no problem walking right out the door and going anyhow. If I wanted to have drinks and not come home, I did that too.

And I had a good time while I was at it. As soon as my house arrest was over, I spent sixty-eight thousand dollars. Not just on shopping for things for myself, but on toys and games and clothes for the kids, and on champagne and treating my friends when we went out to eat at my favorite restaurants in Memphis, like Spindini. I figured they deserved to be spoiled a little since they'd stood by me—unlike *some* people.

Around that time, I stopped making such an effort to go see John play golf too. John and his agent tried to use this against me when we eventually got divorced, saying that I missed flights that had been booked to take me to tournaments. Of course I missed flights, and I didn't care if he lost the money on tickets either. During this period, John was drinking all of the time, gambling, playing so bad that he wasn't winning tournaments or even making cuts, and running around with other women. When I called and checked his voice mail, there were always messages from girls he could never answer for, saying they had just been around the night before. So, no, I wasn't going to fly in to meet him at the tournament on a Thursday, like he wanted me to do, and play house and do the family scene, after he hadn't answered his phone from Sunday to Wednesday. And, yes, I was probably at Spindini partying my ass off instead of being with him, but, you know, I did my part with the kids, getting them to bed first. I was handling my stuff. For once, I decided he could handle his own stuff, without me making everything okay for him. I was done pretending.

It's no surprise that we'd both had enough by this point, and on October 17, 2006—three years to the day after the first time—I filed for divorce again.

Someone described this in a news story as a race to the courthouse. And that was a pretty accurate description. When I told John that I was filing divorce papers, he told me that he'd been planning to file too. Now, I know it doesn't really make a difference who's the defendant and who's the plaintiff in a divorce case. It's always a sad, hard time, especially for the kids, and it always works out the same in the end. But I was determined that I was not the defendant. After everything I'd been through, when it came to this divorce, I was the plaintiff.

But John and I weren't quite ready to let go of each other yet, or maybe we had both gotten hooked on the roller-coaster aspect of our relationship. The divorce papers were hardly filed before we decided to try to work things out one more time.

I think I was also getting used to how crazy life with John was, and so stuff that had seemed unacceptable to me before was just another quiet day around the house. Looking back at some of the things that didn't faze me then, they seem pretty scary. But I was immune. Not long after we decided to reconcile, we were staying up at the house in Dardanelle, and we had some neighbors from Memphis there with us too. We were sitting in the clubhouse at the golf course John owns there, having a little party, when my neighbor and I heard this loud noise outside in the parking lot. We looked at each other.

"What is that?" she said.

I should have been able to tell her, without even looking, that it was probably the sound of John doing something totally nuts. And when I peeked out the window, I saw that it was. John had this Hummer golf cart, and he was running it into my Mercedes, again and again and again, just denting it all up and scraping the paint and everything. Remember how he had that nickname for me, "Queen" or "Queenie"? Well, I had a tag on my car that said "Queen Bee," which he had completely dented by the time he was done crushing my car. He thought he was being hilarious when he hung the banged-up tag on the wall for a souvenir.

ten

I'M NOT
GOING DOWN LIKE THIS

I HAD GOTTEN SO USED TO living in chaos that I was able to deny for a while that things were getting worse. As usual, John always thought that a trip or a change of scenery would clear up any negative feelings that lingered between us after he'd done something bad. And so, in January of 2007, I agreed to go along to Hawaii for a tournament. On the way, we made a quick stop in California. Now, he had promised that if I would fly out to California and bring the kids, he would not drink any whiskey because I told him it was the only way I was going. I left Little John at home with my mom and dad, but Austin came with me. When we got into town, John took us out to dinner, which was kind of a big deal, since he knew I liked to go out and he never would. Only, when the waitress came over to the table, he ordered a vodka orange juice. I gave him a look.

"That's not whiskey," he said.

"Yes it is, John," I said. "It's the same thing."

But, of course, he did what he wanted. I swear he drank ten of these drinks. I wasn't drinking, because I never, ever drank around him at that point in our marriage, and I was just fuming because I'd barely gotten into town and he'd already broken his promise. Plus he was getting drunk, and I was going to have to deal with that nightmare too. I made up my mind that I was going to leave for home the very next day, because if he was going to break his part of the deal, then why should I honor mine?

And then it got even worse. Because John was famous, people were always kissing up to him. They thought it made them look cool if they gave him drinks and enabled his bad behavior. It used to make me furious. People knew that he didn't need to drink whiskey and that he'd done crazy things and torn up rooms, and yet they loved to help him to be this big mess. Well, this time, the stupid waitress came over. She was giggling when she set down his drink.

"We're out of orange juice, so I just brought you the vodka," she said.

It was basically a whole big glass of vodka on the rocks for somebody who's already a nut. And I was sitting here thinking: *You don't have to go home with him. Why are you doing this?* So then I really fumed. But I didn't say anything because I knew better than to get into it with John when he was drunk, because he'd just start tearing everything up, which he might do regardless. I figured that even if I couldn't prevent it, at least I could not cause it. But it didn't matter because, when we got back to the bus, I told him that I was going back to Memphis in the morning and he went completely crazy. He grabbed me by my hair and he literally started ripping it out in chunks.

"You're not leaving me," he said. "I'll *kill* you if you divorce me!"

And the whole time that he was yelling at me, he held on to my hair and beat my head on the bus walls. All I could think about was how I could get out of there, and I tried to scramble away from him. Well, he grabbed on to me by the front of my bra, and he tugged on it so hard that it ended up leaving bruises around my ribs, and then it finally broke. I started screaming for Austin, who mercifully had slept through all of this and was still asleep in the front of the bus.

"Call the police!" I yelled. "Call the police!"

When John heard that, he took my cell phone and broke it into a million pieces. Finally, while he was distracted, I managed to get away from him. I ran off the bus, which was parked in the TaylorMade parking lot. We were there because John was signing a $1.8 million dollar endorsement deal the next day, and there he was, drunk and trying to kill his wife in his new sponsor's parking lot.

As I was running, I was thinking about how glad I was that I'd left Little John at home in Memphis, and I knew that, no matter how mad John was at me, he'd never do anything to hurt Austin. Then I started thinking about whether or not I should report John for domestic abuse. But we'd just bought this new house, and John was supposed to pay it off with that deal. If he lost his contract, we'd lose the house, and then I didn't know what would happen to us or how I'd take care of the kids.

So I ran out in the woods, and I stayed out there for what felt like forever. Finally, I figured he must have sobered up and calmed down some. I snuck back to the bus, and from the outside it was still and dark, so I opened the door and climbed back on as quietly as I could. Well, as soon as he saw me, he went right back into a rage and reached for something to throw. I got away from there as fast as I could and ran back to where I'd been. I was huddled against this tree, just sitting there, crying and feeling scared and alone. My head was aching and my scalp was tender and raw. When I say he ripped my hair out, I mean I actually had bald spots throughout my hair, where my head was bleeding. I couldn't just sit there anymore, so I got up and walked around to warm up. I found these steps that led down by the highway. I considered trying to find a ride to somewhere safe. I was so miserable and cold and tired. All I wanted to do was take a shower and climb into a warm bed. But I knew that if anyone picked me up, they'd take one look at me—besides the way my hair looked, by this point I had mud all over my white sweatsuit—and call the police. I didn't want any more trouble. I was still proud, and I thought: *I'm not going down like this*. So I went back to the woods and huddled under a tree all night. I think I was literally out there for nine hours. When it got light, I went back to the bus because I didn't want anyone from TaylorMade to see me looking like a crazy, beat-up woman when they drove into work in the morning. This time John had finally come to his senses. He and Austin were sitting in the front of the bus, having breakfast like nothing had happened. When John saw me, he got up and came rushing over to me.

"Oh, Sherrie," he said, taking in how he'd hurt me. "I'm so sorry. I can't believe I did this to you."

I just walked by him and went into the back to take a shower, so we could try to get on with the day and not freak out Austin any more than we already had. John went ahead and signed that contract. And right after that, we went to Hawaii. John did his usual thing of raining money down on me to try to make up for his actions. I went to this fancy beauty supply store and I bought something like $200 worth of special vitamins that were supposed to make my hair grow, and Frederic Fekkai conditioner, and everything I could find to try to cover up what he'd done. That whole time, he was just shucking out money, and Austin and I were spending it. Anything we wanted, we got for ourselves on that trip. While I was there, I went into a store that sold native Hawaiian arts and crafts, and I saw this beautifully carved wooden mask. I fell in love with it right away. When I asked the clerk about it, he told me it was to keep evil spirits away. I felt like I could use a little bit of that kind of protection in my life right around then, so I got it. I don't think John even asked me what it was, and I don't know what I would have told him if he had.

In the back of my mind, I couldn't stop thinking about what had happened. He had cursed me out plenty. By that point in my marriage, I was good and ready to never hear the word "cunt" again, especially not directed at me. And he had destroyed millions of dollars' worth of stuff around me, if you added up all of my jewelry and cars and every time he had torn up the bus and our houses. But other than the day I choked the strippers, he had never been violent with me. I was wondering what had changed. I think I knew deep down inside that it wouldn't be long before I left him for good, even if I wasn't feeling quite strong enough to make the break yet. And I think he knew it too. It wasn't surprising that a man who threatened to kill himself when I left him alone to go to dinner would really go nuts when he thought I was leaving him for good. It was almost like, if he couldn't have me, he didn't want anyone else to either. In a blind rage that night in the TaylorMade parking lot, he had wanted to kill me. But, really, that wasn't John. He couldn't kill me. It wasn't in his nature. So somewhere deep down inside of him, he started hatching a plan to make sure nobody else would ever want me. Or at least I think that's partly the explanation for what happened next. But John was getting so crazy by this point that it was hard to find reason in anything he did that year.

His Boys and Girls Clubs charity event in Arkansas that Memorial Day weekend was the usual disaster that I'd come to expect. We had around a thousand people there, including my family and a bunch of our friends and neighbors from Memphis. One of the highlights from that year was John pissing on the barbecue grill. I'm surprised people even came over to our house anymore by then. I was still inside getting the kids organized with the babysitters. I hadn't even been outside to welcome everyone, yet he was already cutting up. Finally, I walked out to the edge of our porch, and it was another case of him getting so drunk that he forgot he was married. There was a young woman in his lap with her arms around his neck. I just stood there and watched, trying to calm myself down by telling myself that she was going to get a picture with him and leave. But she didn't. The rage was just rising in me. I could see my parents down on the lawn and I didn't want them to know what was going on. Luckily, my dad is blind in one eye, and he can't hear anything. My mom was sitting beside him, but all she could notice was the barbecue she was eating. So I figured I could take care of this without them even being aware of it. It wasn't like I was going to throw the girl on the ground and start beating her up, like I wanted to do. I walked up and tapped her on the shoulder.

Tap. Tap. Tap.

"I need you to get out of my husband's lap," I said.

She looked up at me and she was not impressed. Her look said: *Get out of me and my boyfriend's face.* Clearly, they *knew* each other, if you know what I mean.

I stood there, waiting. She didn't move. I tapped her one more time.

"Now," I said.

That was it. I snapped. I grabbed her by her shirt and moved her myself. My dad finally looked up and saw what was going on. He turned to my mom.

"Billie, I think you need to get your daughter," he said. "She has a girl all jacked up."

I had her all twisted up by her shirt, and I took her over to security.

"Get the fuck out of here," I said. "I'm over it. Just get out."

Well, she was as drunk as John was, and she started staggering back to get in John's lap again. John was so wasted that he was just sitting there like, "Huh?"

So I just gave up. I went over to him and tried to get him to focus on me.

"You have a good time at your party because I think I'm going to leave now," I said.

Everyone had seen all of this go down. I went into the house and got the kids ready to leave. So John did his usual. As soon as he started causing a scene, I hurried the kids out to the car because I knew that my windows were next, and I was not planning on driving home to Memphis, like I usually did, with no glass in the windows. I didn't even take the time to tell my friends I was leaving. I called them from the car.

"Y'all, I'm gone," I said. "I'm just going to have to head home to Memphis."

"We're right behind you," my neighbor said.

"Great, can you get my purse?" I said.

That's how fast I had left.

John ended the party drunk and passed out in a heap on the floor, the whole house torn down around him. No one was surprised anymore. But I wasn't the only one who was getting fed up. Sometimes it's the little things that make us snap. My mom and dad were staying with us in Dardanelle during that trip, and my dad is real particular about his groceries. He's always got to have a certain brand of the things that he likes, especially his orange juice, even when he's traveling. So they'd gone to the store and gotten all of his favorites and put them in the fridge. Well, John tipped the fridge over in the middle of his mayhem, and all of those nice new groceries went everywhere, including the whole carton of orange juice. For some reason, that was the final straw for my dad.

"I'm never coming back up here," he said. That was no small thing, since he really did love John like a son. But he was done.

I wish I could say the same thing for myself, but I forgave John once again. Life returned to normal—or what was normal for us then, which could be counted on to include plenty of chaos. It should have been a happy season for us. It was time for the St. Jude

Classic again, which meant it was exactly six years since we'd met. We owned a nice home in the Southwind complex, so it could have been a real relaxing tournament for John, staying at home, just going over in the morning for the day's play. And it started out nice enough. Wednesday was a pro-am day, and I caddied for John to raise money for St. Jude. I carried his golf bag for eighteen holes, with someone donating a thousand dollars for every hole, and John and I had a fun time together. Then, after he was done playing on the first day of the tournament on Thursday, he and I went and picked out a new house in a really upscale neighborhood near where we lived, in order to try to make a new start together. We finished the night by bowling with some friends. But then, when we got to the gate that we had to drive through to get to our house, the gate didn't work like it was supposed to. And even though John wasn't drunk, he just snapped. He got out of his car, was incredibly rude to the guard, broke the gate off, and threw it on the ground.

I was so embarrassed. I saw these guards every day, and they watched out for us and were always so sweet to our kids. Not that John knew this, because he was never at that house. So then for him to come to our home and cause friction with these people who were good to us, it really made me mad. I don't treat people that way. I've always treated the garbageman the same way I would treat the president, and I couldn't stand to think of John behaving like these guys were our servants or something. I was mad, and there was no way I was sitting around the house with him all night when he was in that state.

"You stay with the kids," I said. "I'm going over to Angela's because I don't even want to see your face right now."

After I'd cooled off at Angela's, I headed back to my house. I called John on my way home, just to see if he or the kids wanted me to bring them anything. Only he didn't answer. His daughter Shynah, who was almost fifteen at the time, did. Apparently, while I was gone, he'd decided he wanted to go out drinking, of course, so he left the kids by themselves and went up to the East End Grill, which was a bar near our house. I knew the kids would be okay with Shynah in charge for a little bit, and after what he'd just done to the gate, I decided to go over to the bar and check on him. I knew they had tables outside on the patio and a whole big scene happening because of the tournament. I wanted to see what he was getting up to behind my back. So I parked my car down at the end of the street and I walked up. And there it was. John was sitting outside and a young woman was sitting in his lap.

I came up behind her and gave her hair a little tug to get her attention.

"I'm here," I said.

She climbed off of him, but no one seemed to think there was anything wrong with what she'd been doing. All of his buddies were there with him, and they were all doing shots of whiskey, thinking that it was all just good fun. I was furious when I saw this. After he'd been playing so terribly, he was finally playing well. He was almost leading the tournament that year, and here were these guys who were supposed to be his friends, sitting up late, drinking with him the night before he had to play. I just went off on everybody.

"How could y'all do this?" I yelled. "You know he's got to play golf. You know he's not supposed to be drinking whiskey. All of you sit up here with him, you buy him shots, you drink the whiskey with him, and he's fun and games up here. But me and my kids, we have to be there when he comes home and tears down the house. So y'all make sure you have a real good time, because he's coming home to drive us fucking crazy. You know what? Why don't you get him to spend the night with you instead?"

And then I walked inside and went straight to the bar.

"Can you give me a ride home?" I said.

A waitress said that she could.

"Okay then, can you give me a shot of Jäger?"

I took the shot and then got a ride straight home. I was always really careful not to drive drunk, and especially that night because I knew John had all of the cops in his pocket. If he was mad at me for making a scene, he'd get them to pull me over, and then he'd find a way to screw me, one way or the other.

I left him up there partying, and I went home. I checked on the kids, put on a facemask and worked some conditioning treatment into my hair, and went to bed. Well, he woke me up a few hours later when he came home, and to this day I still don't know what got into him, but he was really raising hell.

The first thing was that he wanted to have sex with me and I didn't want to, not after he'd been drinking like that and we'd been fighting.

"I'll have sex with you if I want," he said. "You're my wife."

He was masturbating and making all of these gross noises and talking about getting with one of his ex-girlfriends. And then he grabbed me and started cramming his hands all over me, and it was basically like he was almost raping me. I tried to push him off but he was so big and heavy.

"Get the fuck off of me!" I yelled.

Luckily he was so drunk that I was able to push him away. This was usually the point when he started smashing stuff, and that was one thing when we were in our house in Dardanelle. But our Memphis house, which I called *my* house, was a smaller house, and if he were to start throwing things and one of the kids walked out of his bedroom, they could get hit with something.

"This is my house," I said. "If you break one thing in my house, I'm calling the police on you."

So, of course, he started breaking stuff. I dialed the police. Really, I was just trying to scare him and make him stop. I handed him the phone so he'd know that I wasn't joking around.

Only when I gave him the phone, he started talking to them.

"My wife's crazy," he said. "She's a convicted felon. She's been hitting me."

I just thought to myself: *Oh dear God, he's going to have me put in jail. It's Friday, and he's going to have me in jail all weekend. I've got to get out of here.*

So I swooped up my kids from their beds and ran out the back door. John's oldest daughter, Shynah, was there, but I figured he wouldn't do anything to her because it was only me that he was mad at. We cut through the yard and went to my neighbor's house. And mind you, I still had a facemask on. My hair was slicked back with conditioner. I looked like a fright. But my neighbor let me in. It wasn't even five in the morning, but I started calling my attorney. He was really worried for me.

"Sherrie, whatever you do, do not talk to any police," he said. "They're going to arrest both of you if you go down there. Find somewhere to stay until I get back."

I was exhausted, so I had my neighbor watch the kids and I went to sleep.

"I'm just going to take a nap," I said. "Don't answer the door for anybody."

Well, of course, her husband's a big ass kisser to John, so he had to run right over to my house and check on John. The next thing I knew, she rushed in and woke me up.

"Sherrie," she said. "Did you cut John?"

"What?" I said. "I didn't touch John. I ran out the back door."

"Well, his face is bleeding," she said. "And the police are down there with him. And some officers came to the door here and I had to give them your kids."

I felt sick when I heard this.

"What?" I said. "One of the kids isn't even his. Austin is mine."

I was so upset and I didn't know what to do, so I called my attorney back.

"Get out of there," he said.

So my neighbor and I went into her garage from the house, and she had me lie down in the backseat. She backed the car up and told me that she could see them all down in front of my house, but they never saw me sneak out with her. She drove me undetected to the home of another friend who's an attorney.

My neighbor dropped me off and I was hysterical and pounding on my friend's door. I don't even think it was six in the morning yet. I'm sure I looked wild-eyed when he answered the door.

"Can I come in?" I said. "John's saying I tried to kill him or something."

"Yeah, get in here," he said. "What's going on?"

"I guess he's scratched himself or cut himself," I said. "And he's saying *I* did it and all of this other stuff."

I was totally distraught, but they were so nice to me. He and his wife, who I'd never met before, and his daughter and their dog were all piled up in their bed, and they were very kindly trying to calm me down. He got on the phone with my attorney, who was literally driving on his way to take part in another trial, but in the meantime he made a few calls for me. After he talked to the police, he called me back.

"Sherrie," he said, "there are scratches on his face, and he's saying you cut him with a knife. It doesn't add up. This is bullshit."

I wanted to be reassured. But I knew that John could be very convincing, and he had my kids, so I was terrified that I was going to be arrested and put in jail, even though I hadn't done anything but run away.

The whole thing was so insane. I never saw John with the scratches because I was hiding to avoid getting arrested. But my dad told me later that he went over to the house to see what was going on and it was just crazy. John had scratches on his face and what was supposed to be blood, but it looked like makeup on his shirt, and he was standing out in front of the house holding Little John. My dad went right up to him and tried to talk to him, man to man.

"John, what are you doing?" he said. "Get in there, get yourself cleaned up, and stop this. What is wrong with you? Those aren't even knife marks. What did you do, scratch yourself?"

"No, Dad," John said. "She tried to kill me."

It was scary crazy. John had lied plenty of times before, but this was something different. I almost wondered if he had gone on a cocaine binge and gotten all paranoid or something. I'd never, ever known John to do drugs, and I'd never accuse him of doing something without good reason, but this actually seemed like a case where there were drugs involved. I certainly don't know how else to explain it.

Even after all of this madness, there was still enough time for John to make it to his tee time, and that's exactly what he did. He went to the golf course that day, with the scratches all over his face, and he played in the tournament. He made a big deal of having all of these cops and armed guards around everywhere, and these heli- copters flying overhead, as if I was going to come out of nowhere and attack him or something. Even crazier, he put Little John in the clubhouse with two armed guards watching him. My poor baby must have been terrified. And I couldn't do anything because I was afraid they'd arrest me and haul me away and I'd never see my kids again. My picture was all over the news, like I was a wanted criminal who'd fled the scene. Of course I'd fled. My husband was a lunatic.

My dad went down there and at least got Austin back. But I didn't know when I'd see Little John again. In the meantime, one of my friends told me that I needed to go get a rape kit done, since he'd been so rough with me, and I did.

Finally, I went down to the courthouse and filed for divorce again, and in the documents I put everything in there: how he'd said he could have sex with me, and even though I was unwilling he'd tried to force me, and that he'd been so rough with me and pulled my hair. I listed everything in there. But I didn't want everyone to know all about my private business, and I kept telling his attorney that.

"I do not want this to get in the news," I said. "Can you please just tell John to bring Little John back? And let's settle this, because this is about to be nasty. I'm about to tell everything on him if it takes that to get my son back. I'm not doing this."

And Gail was calling John, telling him he needed to stop this charade. But he would not stop. He was just taking his lie further and further. Finally, the Shelby County cops must have suspected that he had faked it, and he was about to get in trouble, so he dropped the charges. What makes me mad, though, is that he didn't get charged with filing fake police reports. And he didn't have to pay for all of the city workers whose time got wasted with all of his nonsense. And, on top of that, no one seemed to hear the part of the story about how it was all lies. All they ever remembered was how I supposedly stabbed him. Because he was a celebrity, and I wasn't, and it was like his word counted more than mine.

While John had been playing at the golf course that first day, I'd decided to make a stand on at least one thing: *I was taking my home back.* I returned to Southwind with Austin, determined not to have to run again. After John dropped the charges, he came home too, and I let him, even though I got some pretty strong advice to the contrary.

We went to a marriage counselor during all of this and told her our story.

"I can't help you," she said. "I think you should get a divorce."

This could have been the excuse we'd been waiting for to finally call it quits, but when we heard what she had to say, we were mad at her. It was almost like we were thinking: *We can hate each other, but you're not allowed to hate both of us.*

John and I walked out to our cars together.

"Was she really supposed to tell us to get a divorce like that?" he said. "I thought she was supposed to help us."

"Obviously, she doesn't think we have any hope," I said.

Truth be told, we did both flip each other off as we were driving away that day, so maybe she was right. But, hope or not, we hung in there.

This may sound mercenary, but John had some really big endorsements at that point that were in jeopardy because of this whole crazy situation, and both of us wanted to save those contracts because they were our family's livelihood. And it was a huge news story. The helicopters were flying over our house that day and they were reporting live: *The Dalys are back in the house together.*

That was probably one of the weirdest moments in our entire marriage. The sound of the helicopters was so loud. And John and I were both lying in bed in the back bedroom. I think we were both exhausted, and we were just talking quietly. Even after everything, John and I actually still got along really well when we weren't making each other crazy. I just turned and really looked at him.

"John, you are so stupid," I said, laughing—not in a mean way, but just because I almost couldn't believe all of this was happening, and I didn't know what else to do. "We have helicopters flying over our house. You are so stupid."

"I know," he said.

"Just tell them the truth," I said.

"I can't," he said. "I'll lose all my contracts."

And I got it. Like I said, I wanted to save those contracts too. And I felt like he had admitted, at least to me, that he knew that he'd screwed up and taken it too far.

"Well, later on, will you please tell the truth?"

"Yes," he said.

But he never did. And that's still the one thing that really gets me mad, and it's the whole reason that I wanted to write a book in the first place. Finally, one way or another, I intend for the truth to come out. I might have done a lot of things I'm not proud of in my life. But I did not stab John Daly.

eleven

MONEY WON, MONEY GONE

VEN JUST LITTLE everyday things became an ordeal. One night I was driving the whole family home from somewhere, and we were caught in all of this traffic on the 240 loop, which cuts through the heart of Memphis. John was drunk and he started carrying on about how he wanted to drive himself to Arkansas. I wasn't about to let him get behind the wheel when he was in a state like that, but he wouldn't let it go. So finally, I reached the point where I was willing to say anything just to calm him down.

"We'll go to Arkansas," I said. "But you're not driving the kids. You're drunk."

He was in that state where there was no talking to him, and he started acting like he was going to open the car door. I was stomping on the brakes, trying to slow down, so that if he did jump out I'd at least lighten his fall a little bit, so he wouldn't kill himself. The car was still moving when he opened the door and leapt out, across traffic, and disappeared into all of the cars. Austin was screaming because it looked like John had been hit by a car. I was trying to reverse down the highway to find him, but there was so much traffic that I couldn't really do anything. Finally, we could just make him out on the other side of the road. We were in an extremely bad part of town and he just started walking away. Well, if he didn't want to go home with me, I wasn't going to make him. And I figured he'd upset the kids more than enough for one day. I drove us back to the house and got them quieted down and into bed. A few hours later, John called me.

"Will you come get me and bring me home?" he said.

"No, I will not," I said. "I'm not waking up my kids and dragging them out into the night. Call one of your friends."

Another night, we went out on what another couple might have called "date night." We got someone to watch the kids and we drove over to the Horseshoe Casino for a chance to spend a little time together, just the two of us, and see if we could have a nice time. Well, we did. John had a few drinks, but he didn't seem like he was about to get all crazy drunk. He sat down at the blackjack table and it was just like the early days, when he was winning all of the time, and I was his Lady Luck. He never lost a hand, and in not much more than thirty minutes he had won $55,000.

I drove us back home, and he seemed like he was in a good mood. But he must have had more to drink than I thought he had. Or that switch in his brain flipped that just made him lose it. I still don't really know.

"You're such a bitch," he said.

"What?" I said.

We hadn't been fighting. We hadn't even been talking. I had no idea why he was so upset. But he was. He kept right on cussing me out.

"All you care about is money," he said.

"What are you talking about?" I said.

"You're such a cunt," he said.

I've always hated that word, and I was so sick of hearing it from him.

"I've been called a cunt for about the last time," I said. "You need to find something else to call me, because I'm over it."

He started twisting around in his seat and I couldn't figure out what he was doing. And then he rolled down his window and I figured he was smoking. Then I heard this noise I didn't recognize. I looked in my rearview mirror, and I saw paper flying everywhere. I thought: *No, he didn't. Did this goof just throw money out the window?*

"John!" I yelled.

I knew the money was in $10,000 wrappers, so that was $10,000 right there. He threw another one. Now I was getting upset: *Oh shit, there goes $20,000.*

The last bunch, he threw at one time. *Oh my God, he just threw $55,000 out the window.*

I drove as fast as I could and screeched to a stop in front of our house.

"You get out of this car or I'm dialing 911," I said.

"Sherrie," he said.

"You're crazy," I said. "Just get out. Go in there with the kids and just leave me alone."

In my mind, I was already making a plan to go back and get the money. I figured that maybe he was stupid enough to throw it out, but I had plenty of things I could spend it on, like how it would put my niece and nephew through college. As soon as he got out of the car, I drove away.

He was so dumb that he went inside and told the babysitter everything.

"Can you stay a little longer, because I need to go help Sherrie," he said. "I don't know what I was thinking. I just threw $55,000 out the window at 385 and Winchester."

She wasn't dumb like John. She was smart.

"No, I can't babysit," she said. "I've got to go."

I'll bet that as soon as she left our house, she called her friends and told them what John did.

I called Gail and enlisted her help.

"I'm coming to get you," I said. "I need some tennis shoes and a jacket. And get two flashlights."

"What are you talking about?" she said. "Have you lost your mind?"

"No, but John has," I said. "Again. You won't believe it. He just threw out all of this money. We're going to go back and pick it up."

"What?" she said.

"I'll be there in a minute," I said.

So I tore into her house and borrowed some clothes from her daughter and we started driving back to where he'd tossed the money out the window. Gail wasn't so sure about my plan.

"Girl, we can't drive this Mercedes out on the edge of 385," she said.

And it's true that it was right at the border of the ghetto. And anyone could have come through there, but I didn't feel like we had any choice.

So we pulled over to the side of the road right where it happened, and there were $100 bills everywhere, all in the bushes along the side of the road and in the vents for the drainage. Gail was driving along the shoulder, real slow, with the headlights on so I could see, and I was picking up the bills and handing them to her. She was stuffing them under the floor mat so they wouldn't blow away. It took hours, and I still didn't get all of the loose ones. I was climbing down into the ditch, combing through the grass and the litter. It got to be really late, and cars were slowing down to check out what we were doing. It was really scary. So I called my mom and woke her up. Of course she was worried right away when she heard from me at such a late hour.

"What is it, Sherrie?" she said.

"Mom, can you and Dad come and park on the side of the road over here so it looks like we have some protection?" I said. "We're out on 385 picking up money."

"What?" she said.

But they did like I asked and came over to help us. By then it was three or four o'clock in the morning and we were still out there picking up money. These guys came walking up, trying to act all casual.

"Get out of here," I said. "Leave us alone. We're the FBI."

I don't know how I came up with that one, but it had been a long night.

"Oh, we thought you might need some help," one guy said.

"No, we've got it all," I said. "We're good."

I knew they wouldn't have given us a dollar if they found it.

I've always been a good detective, and I combed every inch of grass along that stretch of the road. I even went under the underpasses and picked up money that had blown down there. It was an all-night job. I managed to collect $22,000 of the $25,000 in loose bills he had thrown out. And then I went over to where the big chunks of money had landed. I thought I knew exactly where they were, and I had planned to get those last because I figured it was easier for other people to take the loose bills. The strategy seemed like a good one at the time.

Well, I never did find those complete wrappers of money. I still wonder if the babysitter's friends got them.

But I felt proud of myself for getting as much as I did. My phone rang as we were getting ready to call it a night. It was John, who was at home with the kids.

"Did you find the money?" he said.

That was the craziest part of the whole situation: We needed that money right then. He had blown a whole bunch at the casino and that was all of the cash we had right then to cover bills and other immediate expenses.

"Yeah," I said. "I found $500."

Maybe I shouldn't have lied like that, since we did need the money. But as far as I was concerned, he was the dumbass who threw it out the window, and he didn't deserve it. So I took that money and put it to good use. I paid Gail's daughter's rent for the year. I paid off a bunch of stuff for my friends and myself. If only I'd thought to put away a little bit of it for the days ahead, but even after everything that had happened, I was trying to pretend like my marriage was still my future.

twelve

THE BIG SURPRISE

T HINGS WERE VERY TENSE that whole holiday season. And John and I really didn't see much of each other. I was basically trying to keep things as normal as possible for the kids while doing my best to stay out of John's way. I had gotten to the point where I wasn't just going to sit around the house and be at the mercy of his moods. And he was drinking so much that he was embarrassing any time we left the house, so I certainly never went anywhere with him. In fact, I had stopped traveling with him altogether. I was afraid to go out on the road with him because I was scared he'd start a fight with me. I was on probation, and so I had to be very particular about what I did and didn't do, especially since I'd seen how far John would take a lie, as he did when he said I'd stabbed him. My probation officer even warned me about it. "You can go anywhere in the world with anybody, as long as it's not John," she said. "I'm so afraid he's going to do something to get you in trouble."

And I figured she had a point. I always knew that because he's a celebrity, they would listen to everything he said and never believe he caused the whole thing.

On New Year's Eve, as had become the norm when we weren't getting along, John was up at our house in Dardanelle and I was down in Memphis with the kids. To welcome in the new year, I went to the casino with Gail, and we met my friend Robin Thizeman there. My phone rang and it was John. I almost didn't answer it, but he was still my husband, and part of me was glad when he called me.

"I really miss you," he said. "I'm really sorry, and I want to work things out."

I remembered how gentle his voice could be. And I felt a little stirring of that old something I used to feel for him. But it wasn't like it was easy for me to trust him or anything he said after what we'd been through. I sat there in the casino, with all the lights flashing around me, and everyone laughing and having fun and celebrating the new year, and I thought about what I should do. The truth was that I still loved him, even after everything, and I still wanted to make it work too.

I felt happy at the thought that maybe it could. I decided that

I was going to load the kids up the next evening and drive to Arkansas to surprise him. I knew he had to be in California in a few days, and he was about to drive the bus out there, so I figured if we could get along, we'd all go to the West Coast with him as a family. We'd do this one more time. Well, we surprised him all right.

So there I was, thinking about how sweet he'd been on the phone and how excited I was to see him, as I pulled up to the house late the next night. There weren't any cars there. It didn't look like there had been a big party going on. And I knew his older daughter, Shynah, was staying there, so I figured they were all asleep in the house. I didn't feel anything weird at this point. So I went around to the back door and I saw that the bed in the master bedroom was all made up and everything was so clean. Well, that was a little weird. But I knew that sometimes we would sleep on the bus when we were getting ready to leave town. Like sometimes, when we traveled a lot, John would just drive off with the kids and me asleep in the back. So I figured they were asleep on the bus. We walked out to where the bus was parked.

The kids went in first. Austin was eight at the time and Little John was four. I came in behind them with our bags on my arms. They went into the back of the bus, and John was in the bed so they were trying to wake him up. I set down some bags and walked back there to join them. John was pretty thick at the time, and he was lying on his side, so his shoulder was up. I leaned down over the bed to wake him up.

"John," I whispered. "John."

And all of a sudden, this girl's head popped up out of the covers. Now, there's not a lot of space in the back of a bus, so we all were very close. And we were so surprised that the kids and I all started screaming.

I started backing up, trying to get the kids together.

"Who are you?" she said.

"I'm *his wife*," I said. "And this is his son. And this is his son. "

He was so stupid. He was wide awake by then, but he wasn't saying anything.

So I took my cell phone out, and I jerked the covers off of them, because I was not going to have him telling me "Oh, we were just lying down, having a nap."

Well, there they were. No pants on. There was her big fat butt, and she was wearing some stupid Arkansas Razorbacks jersey of his, which he knew I would never wear.

By then, the kids and I were really screaming.

I pointed my cell phone at them.

"What are you doing?" she said.

"I'm just taking a picture of you in bed with my husband, that's what I'm doing," I said.

I took my picture, and John still hadn't said anything, so that was that. I started walking backward out of there.

"Get in the car," I said to the kids. "Just go get in the car."

But that wasn't all. The near-naked stranger in bed next to my husband happened to be black. And the thing about John was, he would make remarks when I was with my black friends.

John said to me, "This is your fault."

I said "What?" Then I looked right at the stranger and said, "I'm a little shocked that he's in bed with you."

She said to me, "He told me that he's getting a divorce."

So I said, "He told you right. He's certainly getting one now."

That made her really mad, and she started cursing me out.

And I walked out. But on the way to the door, I saw this cell phone charging in the front of the bus, and I thought to myself, *Oh no, this bitch has set up camp in our house*. We lived on the bus so much that it really was like our home. So of course, I took the phone and stuck it in my bra.

By this point, I was hysterical, shaking and crying. But I knew I had to have proof, so as soon as I got outside I called Gail. "I'm about to forward you some messages," I said. "Just don't even ask. I'm going to explain it."

I don't even know how I drove the car because I was shaking so hard. But I got us on the road and I turned to the kids. "Put on your seatbelts," I said.

I got down the street a little ways, and then I pulled over to go through her phone. It made me mad because I quickly discovered that everybody knew about her. John's friend Johnny Lee, who had been around the whole time we were married, and who I considered a friend too, had sent her a text about how they were looking forward to seeing her. I found out later that she had been at our house and at my sister-in-law's restaurant. John was telling everyone she was a lawyer he had working for him, and I knew nothing of it.

Of course there were messages to him in her phone. And she had sent him a picture of her vagina. Well, just about the time that I saw this, it got even better. I'd just walked in on John in bed with someone, but he didn't call the police and say, "Look, I'm worried about my son. My wife's hysterical; just make sure they're okay."

But he did have the cops pull me over in Dardanelle. They came up to the window.

"Can I help you?" I said.

"We just got a call from John Daly's house. There's been a cell phone stolen and he's going to press charges. He wants it back now."

"Well, I'm Sherrie Daly, and that's my house too, and I haven't stolen anything from my house. How do you steal something from your own house?"

"I just need the phone," the officer said. "I'm not going to be able to let you go. I'm going to have to take you to jail if you don't give me the phone."

So I called my attorney and told him they were trying to arrest me.

"Tell them to take you to jail," he said.

So I turned back to the police officers and just smiled as big as could be at them, showing them that they couldn't get the best of me.

"Go ahead, take me to jail," I said. "Go ahead."

They went back to their car, and when they came back they were real nice.

"No, no," I said. "You've scared my children. I'm upset. You're harassing me. Let's do this. Take me to jail. I'm ready to do this."

"No, Miss Daly, just go ahead," the officer said. "You're fine."

"No," I said, until they were practically begging me to just drive away.

So, anyhow, I ended up leaving with the phone stuck in my bra. As soon as I got out of eyesight of the cops, I just lost it. I knew that John had done a lot of terrible things in our marriage, and I knew that he had cheated on me before, and plenty. But this was different. I had seen it with my own eyes. And he had made me feel like we were working it out by saying that he missed me and wanted to see me, and then he'd gotten caught like that, and in front of our son too. I was tired of being played as the fool. But I was still grieving my marriage too. I drove home, crying and shaking the whole way, and by the time I got back to Memphis, it was around four in the morning. But all of my best friends were there waiting on me: Jennifer Miller, Big D, and Gail. They're all really good on the computer, so in no time at all, we had the girl's mother's name, where she lived, who she was, everything.

And then I had an idea. I took her cell phone, and I went through every phone number she had in it, whether it was her boss, her preacher, or her parents. And I sent them the picture of her coochie with a note that went something like this:

"This is the vagina of the woman I just found in bed with my husband. Me and my children did, actually. I thought you might want to know that she felt this was important to give to my husband. It sounds like she's a very nice girl."

John kept calling and calling me, getting more and more upset as the day went on. I guess the girl was talking to people who were telling her they had just gotten a picture of her coochie in their inbox.

"Sherrie, you've got to stop," John said. "She's an attorney. She's going to press charges. You're going to jail for this."

"That's fine," I said. "Go ahead. I'll break my probation. Send me on to Judge Biggers. I'm going to say, 'Yeah, I've got the picture of the vagina my husband had in his phone. Sure, I sent it to everybody. Send me to federal prison. I'm ready to go.'"

I just kept sending it. It was so much fun. In fact, I even sent it to some people from John's life too. I attached it to a text I sent to John's agent Bud Martin, which said something like this: "Did you share everything with John and will you get ten percent of this?" That one was real funny, because when we were in court fighting over child support, Bud's testimony went something like this: "The attachment to the text message was an up-close photograph of a vagina." It was true. It was an up-close photograph of a vagina. And he deserved it too. I was mad because he was a part of the outings John had brought her along on, and he knew about it the whole time. I was just about done with people keeping John's secrets for him. It was time for all of it to come out.

If that story isn't the final proof that I'm crazy, at least when it comes to John Daly, this one just might do it. After things had settled down, John called me. He said that he had meant it when he wanted to reconcile, and that he knew he was a sex addict who needed serious help, and that he would get therapy if I would agree to give him just one more chance and try to work things out. And I agreed. Everything John had done had convinced me that there was something seriously wrong with him. I'd known this for a few years at this point. But he'd never admitted it. When we'd gone to therapy before, little as it did, it had been marriage counseling. By this point, it was like we didn't even have a marriage left to work on. If we were going to get back together, things had to change on a deeper level. And if John was ready to see this too, then maybe it could happen, especially since he was going to have to be the one who did the work. In the meantime, I was looking out for myself. Something about seeing John in bed with that woman had finally brought it home for me that John didn't have my best interests at heart. And, sadly, he didn't have our son's best interests at heart either. I had to start pushing a lot harder if I was going to get him to do right by our family and me. And so that's what I did. I pushed back.

thirteen

MAKING THE CUT

Divorces are nasty. And boring. Well, in the same way that golf's boring. There are long stretches that are super tedious, where the time seems to drag on and on, and nothing much happens; and then one little thing decides it all. Of course, in a divorce there's also tons of paperwork and big words. And then there's all of the nasty stuff being done behind the scenes. But I guess golf has plenty of tawdry secret happenings too. Anyhow, I'm not going to go into everything that happened with John during the time that it took for our divorce to go through. But I can say that he basically spent the next two years doing the legal equivalent of what he had done to me during our entire nine-year marriage: insulting me, trying to control me, and, when he didn't like me standing up to him, ignoring me.

I don't think John and I ever officially got separated. I don't know what we were. Just not together anymore. He was supposed to be seeing a therapist about his sex addiction. But because he was off traveling around to tournaments, I didn't really know what he was doing. So, one night, I was sitting at home alone, as usual, and I decided to Google him. This news story came up about how he was playing a tournament in New Orleans, and it mentioned that this woman who worked as a promotional director for Hooters had been interviewed, and she said that she was traveling with him on the bus.

I called him immediately.

"So, that woman from Hooters, is that your therapist?" I said.

Apparently that was John's idea of sex therapy. He just picked up this old Hooters girl and took her on the road with him. Over the next few months, she started living with him, answering my home phone and being filmed on his reality television show with him, where he talked about how great their sex life was and how she was his best friend, and he didn't want to marry her because marriage ruins the best friendships.

The more I watched him all over his new girlfriend on his stupid TV show, the more my blood boiled. So I sent him a text. Now, when I can't control myself and I start sending out texts or leaving messages, I go ahead and tell on myself early to my attorney. He's never happy about it, but at least he's prepared for the worst. This

198

one wasn't too bad, though. I didn't use any cuss words or make any threats.

It went something like this: *"You say she's your best friend. I was your best friend until you started screwing everybody and drinking whiskey and pissing in the bed."*

His reply just made me angrier: *"Tell Little John I love him."*

I was like: *Yeah, if you really love him, when was the last time you saw him?* So we did the back and forth like that for a while, as I know a lot of couples do when they're breaking up and there are still emotions involved.

During this time, John completely cut me off, but he wasn't in any hurry to finalize the divorce. It took me more than a year to get temporary child support, and all of the court dates were always being postponed. I never got a prenup hearing, which was all I really wanted because I felt like I'd been done so wrong in that whole deal. He let our utilities get shut off six times. He let them foreclose on the Memphis house, which was the only thing that had my name on it. When they did foreclose, he didn't give me any money or assistance of any other kind. I had no movers. Luckily, my brother and his friends helped me with the big stuff. And then my friend had to call up an old boyfriend from 2001 to come help us move the rest of the stuff because I had to be out the next day, or else they were going to put all of our stuff out on the curb. And I didn't want to lose all of my belongings on top of everything else that had happened.

John had enough money to lose hundreds of thousands of dollars at the casino, and he even paid back markers worth around a half-million dollars during that time. But when I finally did get child support for Little John, it was only for $1400 a month. Then, when our divorce finally went through in 2010, and I was given our house at Southwind, he got in trouble with the IRS and they put a lien on it. Thanks, John.

Mostly I wasn't surprised by anything he did, and I was just happy to be getting my life back. But there were two things that I never could abide. During this time, every so often, I'd hear John in the press talking about his charity work for the Make-A-Wish Foundation, and how much he loved kids, and it would make me want to get sick in my mouth. Maybe he loved kids in theory. But he sure didn't act that way in practice, especially not with his own kids, who he should love the most.

In 2009, Little John had to get tooth surgery, and I needed John to pay around $1400 for the procedure. I certainly didn't have any money. I couldn't even pay the electric bill to keep the lights on at my house. I called our place in Arkansas, where John was living, and tried to get him to help me. But of course, old Hooter controlled everything, and she wasn't about to let me talk to him.

"I need to talk to John," I said.

"I'm going to be the fifth wife, and you need to stop calling here," she said.

I mean, who says things like that? Everyone had said *I* was a gold digger. She's the one who had her first kid with the heir to the Outback Steakhouse fortune. There was even a big court case about it. Supposedly she told him to take the condom off when they were having sex because she said she couldn't get pregnant. And she's so trashy. I mean, really, I know that I can be trashy, but this is a whole different level.

But I tried to stay focused. All I really cared about was my kid.

"You're at my house, bitch, and that's my husband, and I need to talk to him," I said. "Little John's going into surgery. I need to talk to John about it."

She hung up on me for three or four days in a row. She had John's cell phone too, so every time I called that number, she'd answer and yell and cuss me out.

Finally, Little John's surgery was about to happen, and I was going to have to get my dad to pay for it if I didn't get through to John. But she still wasn't letting me talk to him, even though he was still technically my husband, and Little John was the son he'd always wanted. Finally, she pushed me too far.

"You know what?" I said. "Yell all you want, bitch, but you will never make the cut. You will never be Mrs. Daly. You just keep on doing what you're doing. You're doing something I would never want to do with him anyway. But his son's going into surgery, and he needs to be there."

Not only was John not there, but he never even knew that his son had surgery. I was never able to get in touch with him. He didn't see Little John for eight months that year, from the time when I caught him in bed with the other girl. So then, when John finally got Little John for a few days, he freaked out and called me.

"Sherrie," he said. "His teeth are gone."

"Yeah, he had surgery," I said. "They took them out."

"Are they going to come back?" he said.

After everything I'd been through over those teeth, I was tempted to say, "No, they're not. We're going to have to get him false ones. Little baby dentures."

But then I felt bad for John because of how this woman was running his life.

"You didn't know that?" I said. "Your girlfriend was hanging up on me, and you were home the whole time. You were in Arkansas, and you could have been there with him."

That whole situation made me really angry, but I truly only hate John for one thing: what he did to his stepson, Austin. At Christmas 2008, after only seeing Little John once that whole year, John decided he wanted to have his son for the holidays. I didn't want Little John to go because John was drinking heavily again, and I wasn't sure what kind of shape he was in. Plus Little John had separation anxiety when he was away from Austin and me. But the judge let him have visitation for the holidays, and so I had to go along with her decision. John came over to the house to get Little John. I looked on the security cameras and saw Austin go out to John's car. When Austin came back into the house, he was real upset.

"What did you go out there and say?" I asked.

"I went and said, 'Dad, can I go too?' And he said, 'No, you can't come. I'm just going to spend time with Shynah and Sierra and Little John.'"

Well, when Austin came into the house after that, he got straight into bed and he just sobbed and sobbed. There wasn't anything I could do to make him feel better. He wouldn't even open any of his Christmas presents on Christmas Day or until Little John came home. And during that whole winter, I could tell that all of these terrible thoughts and feelings were just eating away at him.

"Why does Dad hate me?" he asked me.

"He doesn't hate you," I said.

But there was nothing I could say to make him believe me, or to make it okay. Austin has never understood why John pushed him away like that. And neither have I. In 2003, when John and I almost got divorced for the first time, an article ran in *Sports Illustrated* in which he said that the worst part about getting divorced from me was that he'd miss Austin so much because he was his first son.

Austin got very depressed and gained thirty pounds, and I couldn't bear to see him so upset. It's one thing if I'm depressed. Okay, boo-hoo for me. I'm depressed. Maybe I won't eat. I'll get too skinny. I'll look like a Q-tip with hair. Whatever.

But when my kid was depressed like that, and it was something I couldn't help him with, it was the absolute worst. I would have liked to have cut John out of their lives completely, to save them that hurt, but I knew that those little boys needed to see their dad, so I tried to make the best of a bad situation. Austin's dad started showing up for him around then, which has helped so much, but John was his dad for five years and that rejection confused and hurt Austin deeply.

In March, after that Christmas, John called the house one day.

"Can I come get the boys?" he said.

"Boys?" I said. "What do you mean?"

"Yeah, Austin too."

"I'll have to ask him," I said. "When they get home from school, I'll ask them and I'll let you know."

So when they got home, I sat them down.

"Do y'all want to go see John?"

"Y'all, like *me too*?" Austin said.

His bag was packed in a second.

Little John was more cautious. He had this expression on his face like: *No way. He didn't want to see me for this long. He left my brother last time.*

"I don't want to go," he said. "I don't want to see my dad."

"Well, he wants to see you," I said.

"I'm not going," he said. "I'm not going."

Obviously, he didn't have a good time when he was there before, but Austin talked him into it. And I was glad that they got to spend the time with him. I knew that as much as I couldn't stand him, my kids needed to see him. It's a real need for them, to get that attention. Little John has a speech impediment, but after he sees John, he doesn't stutter as much. It's like a little fix, even if it's just the one time.

To be totally honest, though, I'm good with John having less influence on Little John's life, other than this great golf talent that Little John already has. It's really weird because you wouldn't believe it could be inherited like that. But after you've watched enough of it, you realize there is a gift. I think Little John's probably got John's talent with Tiger's discipline. I think Little John could be really good. When I see another little kid swinging, they'll be swinging the club all over their heads and everything, while Little John's just chipping them in. So he's got that.

The other good thing to come out of this whole nightmare is that it has made me so much stronger and more self-reliant. Like when the utilities kept getting turned off, I got tired of borrowing money from my parents, and so I learned how to turn them right back on again using the meter on the side of the house. I had a generator set up out back too, and I'd be outside putting oil in the thing to keep it going. Mind you, we were living in one of the nicest neighborhoods in Germantown, which was one of the best suburbs of Memphis at the time, in what was basically a $1.6 million house. It looked like something out of *Gone with the Wind*, with these big white pillars out front, and we had this chugging noise coming out from behind it twenty-four hours a day. But my neighbors were so kind about that. They never said a thing. And then John got us foreclosed out of there anyhow, so they didn't have to deal with us for too long.

After letting things drag on for two years, in February 2010, John decided he wanted that divorce to go through *now*. I don't know whether it was because all of the Tiger stories had come out, and suddenly it wasn't looking so good for him to be traveling around with his mistress on his reality show while his wife was sitting home in the dark with his son. Or maybe it was because of something that was happening behind the scenes. Right around then, I got a call from someone at the Golf Channel, saying that old Hooter was pregnant with twins. I never heard anything more about that afterward, though, so who knows?

Well, out of the blue, we were ordered to go to mediation. And then, after only one day, when John was ready, we had to settle, even though I wasn't ready. The thing that was really bothering me was this clause that said I couldn't write a book or talk to the media, because John had broken the promise he'd made to tell the truth about what really happened the night he said I stabbed him. If I got nothing out of the divorce, I was going to get the right to clear my name, and I fought for it. John was very dismissive of the whole thing. He had the attitude that no one would want to talk to me anyway. That's fine. I finally got to tell my side of the story, and that's all I cared about.

Right after the divorce, John was in the news a lot, and they were saying he was having a comeback. I haven't seen it yet, but I honestly hope he does. Even after everything, I only want the best for him. I remember when I saw the photo in the paper from the night he was taken into protective custody after they found him all drunk and passed out in front of the Hooters, I just sat there and cried.

"Oh, John, what's happened to you?" I said.

I loved that man a lot, for a long time, and he'll always be my son's father, no matter how I felt about him during our divorce. And I never wanted to have to see him brought down so low like that. I do think he can come back, if he starts living right and gets some better karma. People often come up to me and tell me that his career is over. I guess they think it will make me happy to hear them say that. But it doesn't. I would never wish that upon anyone. And I think they're wrong anyhow. Because when John gets ready to play golf, he will win.

I just realized something wonderful. Whether he wins or not, it's not my problem anymore.

Mostly, I'm just glad that I don't have to watch any more golf, especially now that I have a real reason to hate the sport. My sons miss that whole world a lot more than I do, and they've already decided that their stepfather should be a professional athlete. Only this time, they think he should be a wrestler from World Wrestling Entertainment. Sounds good to me. But not really. I'm ready for a little peace and quiet in my life, and the chance to hang out with a higher class of people. Sure, professional golf includes some of the kindest people, who are still my friends to this day, but I can't say the same for all of the screwed-up golfers out there. I thought I was marrying into a world of neatly pressed collared shirts when I married into the PGA; more like a world of dirty laundry. Now that I'll never have to walk another golf course, I'm more than happy to toss out my tennis shoes forever and strap my Donald Pliners back on. At the end of it all, I still hate golf, but my head is higher than ever before, and so are my heels.

ACKNOWLEDGMENTS

My heartfelt thanks to all of my friends: Alex and Trent, Amy C., Amy S., Angela and Brett Hirsch and the whole Lewis family, Becca (a great friend and the best nails in the world), Cathy and Jamie Daly, Gail, Gina and Sadler Bailey, Heather Dawson, Jennifer Miller, Jenny, Jim Hagmire from Limo Express, Kathy and John Sisinni, Kim and Shawn Snipes, Leanie, Leslie and Robert, Lydia, Marci, Mary, Mary Ellen, the Munn family (for always helping me and the kids), Nicole Merrill, Shelly, Susan and Mickey Bradley, Tracy.

Thank you to John Daly for the good times, giving me the opportunity to see the world, and my beautiful son.

ACKNOWLEDGMENTS

The Hardy family and 84 Lumber for being there for my whole family through all the hard times.

Chip Linebarier, D.D.S., for keeping my teeth in great shape while I traveled the world two times.

Marnie Klyman for guidance through tough times and putting me in contact with a great therapist.

Kent Davis with First Capital Bank for all the loans, and Regions Bank for giving me those four months before putting me out on the curb.

Bret Saxon and Doug Ames for helping me get the book done.

My attorneys, Leslie Ballin and Randy Fishman, and the whole staff at Ballin, Ballin & Fishman for all of the patience and hard work, and for taking my calls at all hours since 1997. George Shaddock. Kemper Durand. Drayton Berkley. And to Arthur Horne III, of Horne and Wells, for all the help, and the great friendship.

And, most of all, I would like to thank Jesus, for getting me through all of the times when I felt like I just couldn't take any more.

Printed in the United States
By Bookmasters